H

The Insan

Volume One: Christianity

Casper Rigsby

The Atheist Republic

This book was published by Atheist Republic, a non-profit organization with upwards of a million fans and followers worldwide that is dedicated to offering a safe community for atheists around the world to share their ideas and meet like-minded individuals. Atheists are a global minority, and it's not always safe or comfortable for them to discuss their views in public.

At the very least, discussing one's atheistic views can be uncomfortable and ostracizing. In some countries, speaking out against religion can put someone in physical danger. By offering a safe community for atheists to share their opinions, Atheist Republic hopes to boost advocacy for those whose voices might otherwise be silenced.

You can sign up for the Atheist Republic newsletter for unique insights and stories from the Atheist Republic community.

Table of Contents

Introduction 7

Chapter 1 : In The Beginning 10

Chapter 2 : More Old Testament Insanity 26

Chapter 3 : The New Testament 50

Chapter 4 : Fundamentalism by Proxy 69

Chapter 5 : Ten Questions 81

    Part One 83

    Part Two 99

Chapter 6 : A Final Plea on Behalf of Sanity . 104

References 111

Author Bio 112

INTRODUCTION

I remember as a child believing in all sorts of weird and crazy things, like vampires and goblins, witchcraft and magic, even government conspiracy theories. As a child these things seemed wholly possible because the world was largely a wondrous and mysterious place for a child. Things like physics and other scientific disciplines that explain why the world is the way it is, were largely unknown or not understood at all by me then. But as I've grown up I've come to see the world as it is rather than how I'd like to imagine it to be. I've come to understand that there are no vampires or witches, no magic, and in all likelihood what we call the supernatural is merely a misunderstanding of nature. In short, when I became a man I put away childish ideas in favor of reality.

Many people however seem incapable of this. As they grow into adulthood they merely trade one fantastical idea for another. They leave Santa Claus behind and adopt god as their new benefactor. Of course Santa is just fiction, but their god must be fact. It doesn't seem to occur to them that these two ideas are merely one in the same. If we examine them closely, the parallels are unmistakable.

Santa has a list of good and bad people. The good ones get gifts and the bad ones get punishment. It's the same with this god fellow as well. If you're a good child you get an eternal pizza party, but if you're bad it's a permanent time out in a lake of fire.

So why is it, that one of these ideas is widely accepted by the majority of people and the other is not? What it boils down to is doctrine. You see, there is no gospel of Santa Claus and as such the tale of Santa is an oral myth that has no definitive writ to follow. Sure, we can go back and see how the myth began, but what does Santa require of his followers? The only thing we know is that Santa supposedly wants us to be good people. But how we are supposed to be good people isn't laid out in a specific doctrine, and so that judgment is left in the hands of the one perpetuating the myth.

When dealing with the idea of god however, we do in fact have set commandments given through doctrine that we are supposedly meant to follow in order to earn our reward from these gods. It is the ideas of these doctrines that I'd like to break down and address here, and how blind faith is indeed a form of insanity. And it is my sincere hope that by the end of this book, you will see these doctrines for what they are… nothing but insanity.

Chapter 1 :

In The Beginning

Section 1

I'll start with the genesis myth of the bible. In the book of Genesis, the bible begins by telling the supposed story of the creation of the universe, and humans.

In the beginning God created the heavens and the earth. Now the earth was formless and empty, darkness was over the surface of the deep, and the Spirit of God was hovering over the waters.

And God said, "Let there be light," and there was light. God saw that the light was good, and he separated the light from the darkness. God called the light "day," and the darkness he called "night." And there was evening, and there was morning—the first day.

And God said, "Let there be a vault between the waters to separate water from water." So God made the vault and separated the water under the vault from the water above it. And it was so. God called the vault "sky." And there was evening, and there was morning—the second day.

And God said, "Let the water under the sky be gathered to one place, and let dry ground appear." And it was so. God called the dry ground "land," and the gathered waters he called "seas." And God saw that it was good.

Then God said, "Let the land produce vegetation: seed-bearing plants and trees on the land that bear fruit with seed in it, according to their various kinds." And it was so. The land produced vegetation: plants bearing seed according to their kinds and trees bearing fruit with seed in it according to their kinds. And God saw that it was good. And there was evening, and there was morning—the third day.

And God said, "Let there be lights in the vault of the sky to separate the day from the night, and let them serve as signs to mark sacred times, and days and years, and let them be lights in the vault of the sky to give light on the earth." And it was so. God made two great lights—the greater light to govern the day and the lesser light to govern the night. He also made the stars. God set them in the vault of the sky to give light on the earth, to govern the day and the night, and to separate light from darkness. And God saw that it was good. And there was evening, and there was morning—the fourth day.

And God said, "Let the water teem with living creatures, and let birds fly above the earth across the vault of the sky." So God created the great creatures of the sea and every living thing with which the water teems and that moves about in it, according to their kinds, and every winged bird according to its kind. And God saw that it was good. God blessed them and said, "Be fruitful and increase in number and fill the water in the seas, and let the birds increase on the earth." And there was evening, and there was morning—the fifth day.

And God said, "Let the land produce living creatures according to their kinds: the livestock, the creatures that move along the ground, and the wild animals, each according to its kind." And it was so. God made the wild animals according to their kinds, the livestock according to their kinds, and all the creatures that move along the ground according to their kinds. And God saw that it was good.

Then God said, "Let us make mankind in our image, in our likeness, so that they may rule over the fish in the sea and the birds in the sky, over the livestock and all the wild animals, and over all the creatures that move along the ground."

So God created mankind in his own image,

   in the image of God he created them;

   male and female he created them.

God blessed them and said to them, "Be fruitful and increase in number; fill the earth and subdue it. Rule over the fish in the sea and the birds in the sky and over every living creature that moves on the ground."

Then God said, "I give you every seed-bearing plant on the face of the whole earth and every tree that has fruit with seed in it. They will be yours for food. And to all the beasts of the earth and all the birds in the sky and all the creatures that move along the ground—everything that has the breath of life in it—I give every green plant for food." And it was so.

God saw all that he had made, and it was very good. And there was evening, and there was morning—the sixth day. – Genesis 1:2-31

In this narrative we are given the idea that an all-powerful god creates the entire universe in just six days mostly by speaking it into existence. Now there are some serious problems with this narrative when weighed against reality. For starters, how can there be days before the sun, earth, and moon were created? Our understanding of days is based entirely on the revolution of the earth and its orbit around the sun. The inherent problem here becomes apparent when we do a bit of math. A day on earth is 24 earth hours, but a day on Mars or Venus or any other planet can be shorter or longer than 24 earth hours. So the problem becomes one of logistics, i.e. we don't have a solid frame of reference. Are we talking about a day in earth time or in gods' time, or measured by some other means? The question becomes, is a day for god the same length as a day for humans? Are we talking about 24 earth hours, or some arbitrary time frame outside of our understanding of given space-time?

This issue isn't some arguing point dreamed up by atheists to try and discredit the bible. It is in fact an issue that has been debated in the theological community for centuries. It is such a serious issue that it's brought division between many Christian denominations. Many biblical literalists in the evangelical Christian community stand firm in the belief that the days listed in Genesis must be interpreted as literal 24 hour earth days, while others such as the Catholic Church proclaim these days to be merely an allegorical reference saying that these days could be anything from eons to seconds and can't be judged by a human frame of reference.

For the atheist this narrative is simply primitive men trying to explain something beyond their comprehension. They did the best they could with what they had to work with and took a stab in the dark because any answer seemed better than none. In this modern age we have real answers to this question, and while it may not be as soothing to the mind and ego as the religious explanation it shows its validity and merit in the world around us. But cognitive dissonance is hard to overcome and the simple comforting answer is the one most choose to believe.

When this new information presents itself and we are given answers that do not fit with our current perception, cognitive dissonance presents itself and we battle in our minds over which ideas to accept. There are many courses of action to take when this happens. The most common reaction is denial. The person will receive the new information and dismiss it flippantly without truly investing any time in substantiating the validity of the idea. It simply doesn't fit with their worldview and so they dismiss it. Secondly, one can integrate the new idea into their current worldview. Take for instance the Catholic Church, who accepts the theory of evolution but contends that it is merely the mechanism god used to make life on earth. They contend that while all life evolved on this planet, at some point god gave humans souls and made us special. The final option when confronted with cognitive dissonance is acceptance. When confronted with conflicting ideas, one can choose to accept the idea which offers more tangible validity than the other. One can be taught that babies are delivered by storks, then later in life they may come to learn how babies are actually conceived and born. They will then have to choose which idea is actually valid and which lacks any supporting evidence to validate it. Still some people will argue tooth and nail in favor of the stork even after seeing their own children born. This is true for this genesis myth as well. Even though we have every reason to doubt the validity of this myth, many still cling to it because it comforts their minds.

Whether it is the literalist who insists that the myth is actual fact, or the more liberal believer who accepts the facts but sees them to be a part of a grand design, one must embrace a certain degree of insanity in order to accept the myth at all. Even the believer who sees themselves as a rational and logical individual must accept the idea that there is a magical world outside of our own where mythical beings like god supposedly exist and there is nothing rational or sane about that idea. The spectrum of belief from the liberal to the fundamentalist is merely a spectrum of insanity from the mildly offset to almost schizophrenic like delusion. It's no different than the functioning alcoholic and the homeless wino. Both are alcoholics, only to differing degrees and with differing impact.

Section 2

Let's get back to the narrative and see just how much insanity one must accept in order to believe this story as literal so we can examine the different levels of insanity inherent in religious belief or faith.

The literalist must accept some very silly ideas in order to believe this narrative as anything other than a work of fiction. As I mentioned earlier we have the issue of days before a sun and orbital pattern is established, but we have another issue with the sun as well. You see, god supposedly creates light on day one but doesn't get around to making the sun until day four. So for three full days, somehow there are not only days to count but also there is light, and all without a sun even created yet. Worse still, god apparently made plants and trees on day three a day before he made the sun. So the entire basic framework of how our solar system is set up in the bible contradicts what we clearly see from science.

We know from looking at nebulae, which are star factories where stars form first in a solar system swallowing up most gas for fuel. We know that planets form through accretion from the solid particles of elements in these nebulae. And we know these things not from an ancient book, but from direct observation and experimentation. Despite the fact that all evidence points to the contrary, the literalist still continues to proclaim the genesis myth as fact and what we can actually quantify and observe as a fabrication meant to turn people from a belief in god.

There are two key reasons that the literalist is so keen on holding onto an obviously false idea and this becomes very apparent when we get to day six and god supposedly creates mankind. In the narrative we're given that god makes man in his own image and in doing so also creates a hierarchy of existence. This is highlighted as god goes on after creating mankind to give him dominion over all the plants and animals on earth. So the hierarchy established starts with god at the top and then man and then everything else. The reason this hierarchy is important to the literalist is that it establishes humans as special and important and it offers justification for humans using the earth and its resources any way we want. The other reason is that if this narrative and the verses that follow are not literally true, then none of the rest of the bible makes any sense or has any sort of even conjured validity. So let's discuss those next few critical verses from the book of Genesis and see just why it all must tie together or it all falls apart.

Section 3

In chapter 3 of the book of Genesis we are told the story of the fall of man and original sin.

Now the serpent was craftier than any of the wild animals the Lord God had made. He said to the woman, "Did God really say, 'You must not eat from any tree in the garden'?"

The woman said to the serpent, "We may eat fruit from the trees in the garden, but God did say, 'you must not eat fruit from the tree that is in the middle of the garden, and you must not touch it, or you will die.'"

"You will not certainly die," the serpent said to the woman. "For God knows that when you eat from it your eyes will be opened, and you will be like God, knowing good and evil."

When the woman saw that the fruit of the tree was good for food and pleasing to the eye, and also desirable for gaining wisdom, she took some and ate it. She also gave some to her husband, who was with her, and he ate it. Then the eyes of both of them were opened, and they realized they were naked; so they sewed fig leaves together and made coverings for themselves.

Then the man and his wife heard the sound of the Lord God as he was walking in the garden in the cool of the day, and they hid from the Lord God among the trees of the garden. But the Lord God called to the man, "Where are you?"

He answered, "I heard you in the garden, and I was afraid because I was naked; so I hid."

And he said, "Who told you that you were naked? Have you eaten from the tree that I commanded you not to eat from?"

The man said, "The woman you put here with me—she gave me some fruit from the tree, and I ate it."

Then the Lord God said to the woman, "What is this you have done?"

The woman said, "The serpent deceived me, and I ate."

So the Lord God said to the serpent, "Because you have done this,

"Cursed are you above all livestock

> *and all wild animals!*

You will crawl on your belly

> *and you will eat dust*

> *all the days of your life.*

And I will put enmity

> *between you and the woman,*

> *and between your offspring and hers;*

he will crush your head,

> *and you will strike his heel."*

To the woman he said,

"I will make your pains in childbearing very severe;

> *with painful labor you will give birth to children.*

Your desire will be for your husband,

and he will rule over you."

To Adam he said, "Because you listened to your wife and ate fruit from the tree about which I commanded you, 'You must not eat from it,'

"Cursed is the ground because of you;

through painful toil you will eat food from it

all the days of your life.

It will produce thorns and thistles for you,

and you will eat the plants of the field.

By the sweat of your brow

you will eat your food

until you return to the ground,

since from it you were taken;

for dust you are

and to dust you will return."

Adam named his wife Eve, because she would become the mother of all the living.

The Lord God made garments of skin for Adam and his wife and clothed them. And the Lord God said, "The man has now become like one of us, knowing good and evil. He must not be allowed to reach out his hand and take also from the tree of life and eat, and live forever." So the Lord God banished him from the Garden of Eden to work the ground from which he had been taken. After he drove the man out, he placed on the east side of the Garden of Eden cherubim and a flaming sword flashing back and forth to guard the way to the tree of life. – Genesis 3:1-24

In this narrative we're given that a talking serpent tricks a woman into eating a fruit and sharing it with her mate. For doing this, god punishes the man and woman by kicking them out of their perfect garden home and making childbirth painful. This narrative, while obviously silly to any rational person, nevertheless is the very bedrock and foundation of Christianity. Without this story of original sin none of the rest of the bible has any validity at all. If this story isn't true then there's no need for Jesus at all. And it's at this point that I must tell you that if you do not believe this story as fact then you have no reason to believe anything else the bible has to say.

So you can see why the literalist has a vested interest in these narratives. One cannot state with authority that Jesus is the redeemer of mankind if they cannot also state with authority that the biblical fall of man is factual. The problem is that the story isn't factual at all and the authority by which these people state it as fact is an unsubstantiated claim that their god is real rather than offering any physical evidence. In the end the only defense a literalist can fall back on is the circular logic that the bible is true because the bible says it's true. In order to parade that idea around they have to embrace a level of insanity that shuts out all contradictory evidence and become a madman raving nonsense in the streets.

That may seem a bit of an exaggeration, but look at men such as Ray Comfort and Ken Ham. These men are by all accounts raving fools who have posited ideas such as that men and dinosaurs once lived together, that dinosaurs were once all herbivores, that the earth is only 6,000 years old, and let's not forget that the banana proves god's existence. Ray Comfort has many people convinced that the only proof of evolution would be a crocodile evolving into a half duck half crocodile hybrid. And these are just the big names out front because there are literally millions of people on this planet who buy every word these men say. Those people buy this nonsense because these men proclaim it in the name of god.

Most people never question the validity of what these men say. They simply accept it because it conforms to their own preconceived notions and personal worldview. When pressed to validate their beliefs most people simply offer that one must have faith. In truth, what one must have is blind faith and a willingness to believe even the most nonsense ideas. And that's the problem really. If you're willing to accept one brand of nonsense, where do you draw the line? If god is real, then why not fairies and leprechauns? There are books about those mythical beings too. Perhaps those deserve our attention.

Section 4

Before we move on to the next bit of doctrinal insanity, I want to take a moment to highlight something. The genesis myth of the bible is not the only genesis myth out there and certainly not the oldest. Some of the oldest creation myths are those of the Egyptians, Sumerians, and Babylonians. These myths predate Christianity and even Judaism by thousands of years. What is also noteworthy is that we see some of the same themes from the Sumerian and Babylonian creation myths reworked into the genesis myth of the bible.

These crossovers and similarities offer us two very different viewpoints. You see, for the believer the similarities are viewed as a validation of their beliefs. They say that god had been trying to give the message to people and those people simply got it wrong. But god doesn't give up and eventually he gets the story conveyed correctly in the form of their doctrine. The fact that their doctrine often offers ideas that are unethical in a civilized society seems lost on these people. How is it that their god supposedly got it right with a given doctrine, and yet that doctrine doesn't measure up to common sense on issues of justice and equality?

How is it that a supposedly perfect god either doesn't know or doesn't believe that slavery is wrong? How is it, that god doesn't believe men and women are equals? How can it be that such a god can condemn shellfish and pork, yet can't cannot level an outright condemnation of rape? How is it that when Hitler committed genocide he was a monster and condemned by religious people the world over, and yet these same people can read of acts of genocide committed either in the name of god or supposedly committed by god himself, and find that to be righteous and holy? Why is it that when dealing with and thinking about god one must set aside our moral and ethical standards? More importantly, I ask myself each day why religious people themselves don't ask these questions?

Chapter 2 :

Some More Old Testament Insanity

Section 1

Okay, so maybe I got a little ahead of myself in that last chapter. Let's backtrack a bit if you will. I think it's necessary to really define and understand what insanity truly is, because many people are easily offended by terms like insane.

Now, when I use the term insane I am referring to the term as defined in the Oxford English Dictionary, which is as follows: "(Of an action or policy) extremely foolish; irrational or illogical". [1] Under that definition, religious belief is surely an insane thing. It is most often very irrational and most certainly asks followers to suspend their logical thinking. Is it logical to believe that a donkey or snake has ever spoken? Is it rational to believe so just because it is claimed as truth in some supposedly holy book?

No. It most certainly isn't. And so, we must admit that religion asks the follower to acquiesce to insanity.

Now, in chapter one, we began discussing some of the insanity from the bible. We haven't even gotten out of the first book, that of Genesis, and already we have a wizard that lives in another dimension making a mud golem, stealing his rib to make a woman, and a talking serpent. You might think things would level out, however the insanity only ramps up from there. As we continue the story we're going to see things go from mild insanity to outright psychoticness very quickly.

We flash forward just a bit to chapter 4 of Genesis and come to find that the mid golem Adam has impregnated the rib woman Eve, and they have two sons named Cain and Abel.

> *Adam made love to his wife Eve, and she became pregnant and gave birth to Cain. She said, "With the help of the Lord I have brought forth a man." Later she gave birth to his brother Abel.*

Now Abel kept flocks, and Cain worked the soil. In the course of time Cain brought some of the fruits of the soil as an offering to the Lord. And Abel also brought an offering—fat portions from some of the firstborn of his flock. The Lord looked with favor on Abel and his offering, but on Cain and his offering he did not look with favor. So Cain was very angry, and his face was downcast.

Then the Lord said to Cain, "Why are you angry? Why is your face downcast? If you do what is right, will you not be accepted? But if you do not do what is right, sin is crouching at your door; it desires to have you, but you must rule over it."

Now Cain said to his brother Abel, "Let's go out to the field." While they were in the field, Cain attacked his brother Abel and killed him.

Then the Lord said to Cain, "Where is your brother Abel?"

"I don't know," he replied. "Am I my brother's keeper?"

The Lord said, "What have you done? Listen! Your brother's blood cries out to me from the ground. Now you are under a curse and driven from the ground, which opened its mouth to receive your brother's blood from your hand. When you work the ground, it will no longer yield its crops for you. You will be a restless wanderer on the earth."

Cain said to the Lord, "My punishment is more than I can bear. Today you are driving me from the land, and I will be hidden from your presence; I will be a restless wanderer on the earth, and whoever finds me will kill me."

But the Lord said to him, "Not so; anyone who kills Cain will suffer vengeance seven times over." Then the Lord put a mark on Cain so that no one who found him would kill him. So Cain went out from the Lord's presence and lived in the land of Nod, east of Eden.

Cain made love to his wife, and she became pregnant and gave birth to Enoch. Cain was then building a city, and he named it after his son Enoch. To Enoch was born Irad, and Irad was the father of Mehujael, and Mehujael was the father of Methushael, and Methushael was the father of Lamech. – Genesis 4:1-18

There are a lot of messed up ideas presented here. First off, why does god look on Abel's offering with favor, but not Cain's? One could argue that god prefers meats to veggies. One could also argue that Abel brought the best of his stuff while Cain just brought whatever. But god's supposed behavior in the face of this should be troubling if we examine it logically. God's lack of pleasure in Cain's offering, is much like a spoiled child at Christmas. Because god doesn't get exactly what he wants, he acts like the petulant child and just shrugs off the imperfect gift of Cain. When a child acts this way, we scold them and tell them that it is rude to impugn someone's gift as being valueless and unwanted. But when this god acts the same way, we excuse him saying, "God works in mysterious ways". The only real mystery however, is why anyone would worship a god who behaves like that.

So then Cain kills Abel because jealousy is a bitch sometimes, and god acts like he doesn't know exactly what happened. He questions Cain about where Abel is and Cain plays the part of the fool as well. But then god claims that Abel's blood has betrayed Cain and is crying out, alerting god that Abel is now dead.

First of all, god should have known Abel was dead because he's supposedly omniscient. And of course, that same omniscience should have told god what was going to happen long before it ever did. This means god should have known Cain was going to kill Abel and could have intervened at any time to save Abel's life. Some will say, that doing so would interfere with free will, but there's a difference between actually doing something to interfere and prodding someone in a general direction.

Now, what I mean by prodding is just some very innocent manipulation. I'm simply suggesting that god could have employed tactics that most of us who are parents use all the time. You see, I have two sons and if both bring home report cards and one makes straight A's and the other has a few B's, I'm not going to belittle the one who got B's by comparing him to my other son and showing favor to one over the other. As a parent, my job is to help my children succeed and you don't do that by diminishing their own self-respect and self-worth. Instead, you look on their efforts with favor and tell them that you know how hard they tried. You then ask them what you can do to help them be more successful. That's what any good parent does because they love their children and want to see them succeed.

But we look at this god, who is said to be the father of all mankind, and what we see is a supposed father who knowingly and willingly creates enmity between two brothers by showing favoritism to one over the other. All throughout the bible, from beginning to end, we see this persistent idea of a god who shows favor and favoritism, often based solely on the arbitrary notion of paternal lineage, to one person or group over all others. We see a consistent pattern of divisive ideas meant to separate one group from another and assign superiority to one over another.

Lastly, in this story we see a god who is an utter hypocrite. God shows his pettiness and pride by showing favor to one son over another, and then has the audacity to stand in judgment over Cain, for Cain succumbing to pettiness and pride manifested as jealousy that turned to murder. And all of this could have likely been avoided had god simply not indulged his own pettiness and pride. The architect of Cain's failure was not Cain, but the god who set him to fail simply to indulge his own pride. God did not look on Cain's offering with favor because in his pride god believed he deserved only the best. He never had to lift a finger to save Abel; he only had to swallow his own pride and check his ego.

Section 2

Let's flash forward just a bit more, after Adam and Eve populate the whole earth. We'll overlook the rather obvious incestuous implications there, and instead move on to god's first of many highly deadly psychotic outbursts.

> *After Noah was 500 years old, he became the father of Shem, Ham and Japheth.*
>
> *When human beings began to increase in number on the earth and daughters were born to them, the sons of God saw that the daughters of humans were beautiful, and they married any of them they chose. Then the Lord said, "My Spirit will not contend with humans forever, for they are mortal; their days will be a hundred and twenty years."*
>
> *The Nephilim were on the earth in those days—and also afterward—when the sons of God went to the daughters of humans and had children by them. They were the heroes of old, men of renown.*
>
> *The Lord saw how great the wickedness of the human race had become on the earth, and that every inclination of the thoughts of the human heart was only evil all the time. The Lord regretted that he had made human beings on the earth, and his heart was deeply troubled. So the Lord said, "I will wipe from the face of the earth the human race I have created—and with them the animals, the birds and the creatures that move along the ground—for I regret that I have made them." But Noah found favor in the eyes of the Lord.* - Genesis 5:32-6:8

Okay. Let's pause for a second and consider what we just read.

First off, I must applaud a man of 500 years of age for both his longevity and for his sustained fertility. Or maybe, it's a bit presumptuous to believe anyone has ever lived that long. After all, there is absolutely zero physical evidence that any human being has at any point in time lived to such an age. In fact, what the physical evidence shows is that a person living in that era, would have been doing well to reach an age of 50 or 60 years, due to disease and normal physical decay. The reality of human life is that, the very oxygen that sustains our lives is also a death sentence. That oxygen leads to decay and deterioration of our cells, and our bodies lose their ability to repair this damage as time passes. The only way to negate this in any meaningful way, would be to defy the laws of physics and the natural laws such as entropy which govern the decay rates of atomic particles. So the only way to get around this problem is to invoke a supposed supernatural or magical force that can act outside of the laws of nature and manipulate those laws.

Then, we're brought into the realm of what is almost undoubtedly fiction, when we're introduced to Nephilim. Now, if the idea of Nephilim sounds familiar, it's probably because you were paying attention in grade school when you learned about Greek and Roman mythology. The reason the idea of Nephilim sounds familiar, is because the idea is simply a recrafting of a much older mythological idea. The idea I'm speaking of is of course demigods.

In mythological terms, one of the most well-known demigods is a figure known as Hercules. Hercules' claim to fame is that he wasn't just any old demigod born of a mortal and a deity, he was the son of Zeus, king of the gods, and born of a mortal woman. That story sounds eerily similar to another story from the bible... but we'll get to that in just a few chapters.

The main point that I want to impress upon you here however, is that this isn't a new idea, and simply stating the idea using different words does not convey any more validity to the idea. The fact is, angels are just lesser deities within Christian mythology, and what we're dealing with here is the notion that lesser deities once came to earth and populated it with demigods of great strength and power of a superhuman nature. If that sounds like nonsense when addressed from the viewpoint of assessing the validity of Greek and Roman mythology, it should by all rights also sound like nonsense when addressing the validity of Christian mythology.

But we aren't done yet, because this story gets progressively less realistic and even more psychotic as it continues. Less realistic than demigods, you ask? Why yes. Even less realistic than that fantasy notion.

This is the account of Noah and his family.

Noah was a righteous man, blameless among the people of his time, and he walked faithfully with God. Noah had three sons: Shem, Ham and Japheth.

Now the earth was corrupt in God's sight and was full of violence. God saw how corrupt the earth had become, for all the people on earth had corrupted their ways. So God said to Noah, "I am going to put an end to all people, for the earth is filled with violence because of them. I am surely going to destroy both them and the earth. So make yourself an ark of cypress wood; make rooms in it and coat it with pitch inside and out. This is how you are to build it: The ark is to be three hundred cubits long, fifty cubits wide and thirty cubits high. Make a roof for it, leaving below the roof an opening one cubit high all around. Put a door in the side of the ark and make lower, middle and upper decks. I am going to bring floodwaters on the earth to destroy all life under the heavens, every creature that has the breath of life in it. Everything on earth will perish. But I will establish my covenant with you, and you will enter the ark—you and your sons and your wife and your sons' wives with you. You are to bring into the ark two of all living creatures, male and female, to keep them alive with you. Two of every kind of bird, of every kind of animal and of every kind of creature that moves along the ground will come to you to be kept alive. You are to take every kind of food that is to be eaten and store it away as food for you and for them."

Noah did everything just as God commanded him.

The Lord then said to Noah, "Go into the ark, you and your whole family, because I have found you righteous in this generation. Take with you seven pairs of every kind of clean animal, a male and its mate, and one pair of every kind of unclean animal, a male and its mate, and also seven pairs of every kind of bird, male and female, to keep their various kinds alive throughout the earth. Seven days from now I will send rain on the earth for forty days and forty nights, and I will wipe from the face of the earth every living creature I have made."

And Noah did all that the Lord commanded him.

Noah was six hundred years old when the floodwaters came on the earth. And Noah and his sons and his wife and his sons' wives entered the ark to escape the waters of the flood. Pairs of clean and unclean animals, of birds and of all creatures that move along the ground, male and female, came to Noah and entered the ark, as God had commanded Noah. And after the seven days the floodwaters came on the earth.

In the six hundredth year of Noah's life, on the seventeenth day of the second month—on that day all the springs of the great deep burst forth, and the floodgates of the heavens were opened. And rain fell on the earth forty days and forty nights.

On that very day Noah and his sons, Shem, Ham and Japheth, together with his wife and the wives of his three sons, entered the ark. They had with them every wild animal according to its kind, all livestock according to their kinds, every creature that moves along the ground according to its kind and every bird according to its kind, everything with wings. Pairs of all creatures that have the breath of life in them came to Noah and entered the ark. The animals going in were male and female of every living thing, as God had commanded Noah. Then the Lord shut him in.

For forty days the flood kept coming on the earth, and as the waters increased they lifted the ark high above the earth. The waters rose and increased greatly on the earth, and the ark floated on the surface of the water. They rose greatly on the earth, and all the high mountains under the entire heavens were covered. The waters rose and covered the mountains to a depth of more than fifteen cubits. Every living thing that moved on land perished—birds, livestock, wild animals, all the creatures that swarm over the earth, and all mankind. Everything on dry land that had the breath of life in its nostrils died. Every living thing on the face of the earth was wiped out; people and animals and the creatures that move along the ground and the birds were wiped from the earth. Only Noah was left, and those with him in the ark.

The waters flooded the earth for a hundred and fifty days. –
Genesis 6:9-7:24

Alright. Let's pause the story again so that I can make something clear.

Young Earth Creationists like Ken Ham, Ray Comfort, and Kirk Cameron have made the claim, and even made small fortunes for themselves based on the claim, that this story of Noah and the flood are factually true. Despite the fact that there is zero tangible evidence to support such a notion, and despite the fact that archaeological and geological data refute the idea entirely, these men still sell this story as a factual truth. And many men and women eat it up.

And of course, it isn't just the Noah story which they claim as factually true. You see, in order for that story to be true, the Adam and Eve story must be true. So in all reality, these men are showing that their entire belief structure is founded on the belief that some very insane ideas are in fact factual truths. We'll dig further into why this is in chapter four of this part on Christianity, when I dive into fundamentalism and progressive liberal Christianity. First however, I'd like to talk about a bit more Old Testament insanity.

Section 3

In the last bit of scripture we're told that a 600 year old man built a giant boat, put his family and two of every animal on the planet on it, at which time god proceeds to murder everything else on the planet, including women, children, and all the animals. The supposed justification for this act, is that god thinks everyone is wicked and evil except Noah. Now, please note that nowhere in this narrative does it offer that Noah's family was righteous or deserving to be spared from the same fate as everyone else. They are only allowed to live because of the wholly arbitrary fact of lineage.

Moreover, we see that god is willing to murder babies because he thinks that they'll grow up to be as rotten as their parents. This idea is actually a recurring theme in the Old Testament as you'll soon see while explore the Old Testament.

Now, for the sake of trying to keep this book under 400 pages, I'm not going to keep quoting entire passages from this book. At over 700,000 words, the bible is a rather massive book and in all honesty the vast majority of what is written there is either entirely insane or at least borders on insanity. So instead, what I will do from here forward, with a few exceptions, is simply to list the bible passage and give a brief synopsis of what these verses say and why they are insane. But before I do this, I want to make it absolutely clear that by no means do I expect you to just take my word for what these passages say. If you aren't familiar with the bible, please take the time to look these passages up in a physical copy of the bible or on one of the many websites where you can read these bible passages absolutely free of charge.

So, we haven't even gotten out of the first book of the bible yet, and we still have a lot of ground to cover before we do. If we jump forward just a bit, we come to chapter 19 of Genesis and the story of Sodom and Gomorrah. In this tale, we learn that supposedly sometime after that flood we heard about with Noah and his ark, the world is apparently repopulated and there have arisen two twin cities. We then learn that supposedly everyone in those cities is an absolutely horrible person and that they're even full of "the gays", which according to the bible is one of the worst things a person can be. So, god sends a couple angels down there to see if they can find even one righteous person and if they do then god won't destroy the whole area. They find this guy named Lot who is fully righteous, which technically means that god should just let the cities be and get on with business. But in the process of all this, as the angels are just hanging out with Lot, apparently a horde of raging homosexuals show up who want to anal rape the angels. This troubles Lot greatly, so he offers them his daughter to violate instead, but the horde just isn't having any of that. So god tells Lot to get out of town with his family before god destroys everything by raining down fire from heaven. Lot does this, however his wife turns around to look at the destruction as they are leaving, so god turns her into a pillar of salt.

I'm not even sure where to begin with this insanity really. Should I start with the idea that once again god is supposedly murdering men, women, and even children, based solely on the fact that god supposedly doesn't like the way they're behaving? Or perhaps I could discuss why it is that god seems to hate homosexuality? Maybe this portrayal of homosexuality and sexual perversion being synonymous with each other? And let us not forget turning a woman into a pillar of salt simply for being a gawker, which some days we probably all wish would happen to the highway gawkers who cause traffic jams by slowing down to see if someone died in a car accident.

Realistically, this whole thing is insane from start to finish. Why did god need to send angels to find righteous people? Isn't he omnipotent and omniscient? And why all the violence from this god? Drownings and raining fire on people is not only brutally violent, but also completely unnecessary for an omnipotent being. He could just blink them out of existence with no muss and no fuss at all, without any violence in the least. Of course, as anyone who has read the Old Testament will tell you, god in that first part of the bible is one psychotically violent dude. Which is what makes the New Testament even less believable, because once we get to that part of the bible, Jesus starts telling people that god is really just a really nice and mellow guy.

Three chapters after this incident with Sodom and Gomorrah, in verse 22 of Genesis, god apparently asks this man named Abraham to murder his son. Now, of course the bible doesn't call this murder because murder isn't condoned unless god does it or god specifically tells someone to do it. Instead, the bible calls this a sacrifice, which is in and of itself highly disturbing. In typical insane fashion, god supposedly sends an angel to stop Abraham from doing this. In religious terms this is considered god testing Abraham's faith. However, in realistic terms this is emotional terrorism, and the only point that fundamentalists seem to be able to focus on is that god stopped this from happening, rather than addressing just how demented and depraved that even asking someone to do this truly is.

Abraham then proceeds to tell all of his tribesmen that god wants them to cut the tips of their penises off. Apparently giving the notion that a pile of foreskins is an adequate alternative to sacrificing (murdering) a child. This removal of foreskins is also apparently something that is meant to distinguish Abraham's tribesmen, known as Jews, from all other people, known as gentiles. I can only assume, although there's no supporting historical evidence to show it, that Jews went around showing each other their penises all the time. Although that sounds insane all by itself, it's no more insane than any of the rest of this nonsense.

Section 4

Now, quite honestly I could stop right here, having only dealt with the book of Genesis, and I think that my point should be very clear. But for the sake of argument, I want to simply list some of the most insane ideas that make up the rest of the Old Testament.

Following Genesis, we have the book of Exodus which contains what I deem to be one of the greatest lies in all of history. In this book we're told that an Egyptian Pharaoh once enslaved the entire Jewish race, until a baby named Moses shows up in a basket floating down a river. Moses is raised as part of the Pharaoh's royal family even though he's actually a Jew. When he finds out he's a Jew he sets about trying to free the Jews from captivity. What ensues from there on is a festival of madness, violence, and utter insanity.

We get told that Moses is asked by god to try and convince Pharaoh to release the Jews, but that god has "hardened Pharaoh's heart" making it impossible for him to do so even if he wanted to. So then god supposedly kills all the firstborn sons in Egypt except for the Jewish ones because the Jews all smeared blood on their doors to let the angel of death know that they are Jews. Here again, I'm forced to ask why an omniscient god needs to be told anything at all or given physical signs to keep him from mistakenly murdering the wrong people.

Following this we have plagues and famine and disease, and at some point Pharaoh says enough is enough and releases the Jews. But, being as this Pharaoh is apparently just as hateful and vengeful as the god this Moses character worships, he sends soldiers after the Jews to kill them. Moses and his newly freed brethren run as far as they can which is up to the shores of the Red Sea, at which time Moses hits the ground with a stick and the sea actually splits in two so that the Jews can just walk to the other shore. The Egyptian troops follow, but then god makes the sea come back together to drown all those troops.

Now, the reason I deem this as one of the greatest lies in history is that, not only is it full of supernatural nonsense, we actually know with very little doubt that the Jews were never at any time enslaved by any Egyptian Pharaoh. There exists not one tangible shred of evidence to support the assertion that Jews were ever enslaved in Egypt, and this fact has honestly become a serious thorn in the side of both Jews and Christians alike. Despite the massive records of Egyptian history that we have, as well as the historical records of neighboring communities, as well as an unprecedented amount of archaeological discoveries in that region, there is not a single bit of evidence that Jews were ever enslaved by Egyptians. And yet, this story is a foundational part of both Judaism and Christianity, and is taught to the followers of both of these religious sects as factual truth. Never mind how insane the story itself is, because the act of perpetuating something that we know is factually false is an act of insanity all in itself.

After this boldfaced lie, we're then told that Moses couldn't figure out how to walk a straight line and so the Jews were trapped in the desert for forty years. During this time, Moses talks to a burning bush, the other Jews build a golden calf to worship, Moses gets the ten commandments and then smashes the stones he wrote them on over the whole golden calf worship thing, and then finally when they get their bearings straight and figure out where they're going, Moses doesn't get to enter this new promised land even after all he did to supposedly free these people from enslavement.

Most of the rest of Exodus is basically an homage to the supposed Jewish conquest of anyone and everyone in the ancient Mesopotamian region, in which god repeatedly calls for genocide against various non-Jewish peoples. I will spare the reader taking up their time going over all these supposed events and will simply offer two more bits of insanity from that book of the bible.

First is Exodus 22:18 in which Moses tells the Jews to murder witches. It should go without saying that this verse is insane not simply because it calls specifically for murder, but more importantly that it implies that witchcraft is a real and literal thing. In all of history there has never been even one valid and verifiable account of witchcraft being a real thing. In point of fact, I would wager that if it were a real thing, that people able to use supernatural powers to manipulate matter, time, and space, would in fact rule this planet with total impunity and would be unchallengeable by anyone other than another witch or sorcerer.

Secondly, in Exodus 35:2, Moses tells his people that god has commanded them to murder anyone who works on a Saturday. Now, I'm no fan of working weekends, but surely making it a capital offense to do so is not a sane and rational thing to do. Of course, the reason Jews aren't to work on Saturday is because that day is god's own personal holiday. Apparently, in his narcissistic vanity, god needs to have people groveling at his feet at least once every seven days, and seeing as how god is a really busy dude with a tight schedule, it has to be on that one particular day. If you don't grovel on that particular day, apparently god wants you dead, but he's too busy to do it himself so he relies on humans to do it for him. But that isn't insane at all.... right?

Section 5

Now, before I go any further I feel that I need to acknowledge something. I'm sure many have noticed that as this chapter has progressed I've become somewhat dismissive in my presentation of these ideas. The fact of the matter is that, on a personal level these ideas aren't just insane to me, they are completely ludicrous. For me to sit here and try to offer rational discourse of an academic nature about these ideas is tantamount to me trying to offer rational discourse of an academic nature on the magical properties of unicorn flatulence. But, I do recognize that such a comparison, as well as the mere idea that the bible is a book of insanity, is most surely insulting and offensive to believers. My aim here is not to insult or to denigrate into ridicule and derision, but merely to make a case against biblical ideas which are so irrational and unrealistic that the only word which can describe those ideas is the word insane.

So, to keep from letting this degenerate to the point of simple ridicule, I want to wrap this chapter up by simply offering a list, with short descriptions, of some of the most insane ideas from the old testament that I've not yet touched upon, and to simply let you the reader come to an understanding of why they are insane on your own.

1. Leviticus 20:9 says that rude and disrespectful children should be murdered.

2. Leviticus 20:10 says that adulterers should be murdered.

3. Leviticus 24:16 calls for death to any who commit blasphemy. Many Christians often criticize Islamic nations which actually implement such practices without actually realizing that Islam is simply falling back on an idea from the bible that was once used to justify the actions carried out during the crusades and inquisitions.

4. Leviticus 26:27-30 lets us know that if you disobey god he will in turn make you eat your own children.

5. Deuteronomy 22:13-14 offers the notion that any woman who has sex before marriage should be stoned to death.

6. Deuteronomy 23:1 tells us that any man whose testicles have been injured or whose penis gets cut off for some reason, should not be welcomed into the congregation.

7. Deuteronomy 25:11-12 offers the very insightful knowledge that according to god, if two men are fighting and one man's wife grabs the other man by the genitals, you should chop her hand off.

8. 2 Kings 2:23-25 tells the story of a bald man who gets made fun of for being bald by some children, so god sends a bear to murder the kids.

9. In the first few chapters in the book of Jonah, we learn about a man who tries to run and hide from god, ends up caught on a boat in the middle of a storm with some friends, proceeds to have his friends throw him off the boat into the sea in order to calm the storm (this apparently works by the way), and who is then swallowed whole by a whale in whose belly he lives for three days before finally coming out of it all totally unharmed.

10. Lastly, we have quite possibly the most insane character in all the bible, in the book of Ezekiel. Ezekiel is said to be a prophet, who was at first a mute who drew pictures on clay tablets and then laid with a piece of metal between him and the drawing for over a year. Once he begins to talk, things get even more bizarre as he shaves his beard with a sword and proceeds to perform a binding ritual by burning some of the hair, scattering some around the town and stabbing it with his sword, and weaving the rest into his clothes. The insanity in this one book alone is so plentiful that one

could write an entire case study on mental illness based on the supposed life and times of Ezekiel.

Now, this is not, by any stretch of the imagination, all of the insanity in the Old Testament. The fact is, the Old Testament is at least 80% pure insanity. Some of these ruler prophets of the Old Testament are so vicious and barbaric that they make Genghis Khan look like a hippie, and were they alive today they'd either be institutionalized or imprisoned. And yet, because these accounts come from ancient times and because these men claimed to be in cahoots with god, millions of people idolize them and call them prophets rather than insane despots. In all honesty, the only reason anyone gives even a second thought about these things is because they come from an ancient time where these claims were not scrutinized and so they remain largely unprovable. Then, you add the approval stamp of the name of god, and suddenly obvious fantasy becomes heralded as fact, which is a whole other form of insanity altogether.

There is a reason that we call religious belief blind faith, mainly it is because in order to follow these insane ideas and not realize they are insane one has to have blinders on, or filter the ideas through fallacious sieves of philosophical paradoxes. When this happens we get men like Ken Ham whose only real argument against the theory of evolution is to say that we weren't there to see it happen. He then claims god was there to see it happen and he knows god was there because the bible says he was. He knows that god is real because god inspired men to write the bible which tells us that god is real. He can go on and on in this endless loop of circular logic for years and he'll never get anywhere at all. And he isn't alone in doing so.

There seems to be this complete inability for religious folks in general, but especially with fundamentalists, to see that their circular argument for god just doesn't work. The notion that god can inspire others to write a book which confirms god's existence, is much the same as me commissioning someone to write a book about how I can fly and the only validation for the claim that I can fly is the book I had someone else write. God exists because god says god exists just isn't a valid argument no matter which way you slice it. Even if we could actually prove god talked to those men that would be something, but in the same vein we have men who say that god talked to and the only way we know that is because those men said god talked to them. Beyond that, we have nothing. Which shows very conclusively that the bible is nothing but hearsay which glorifies and promotes insanity.

Chapter 3 :

The New Testament

Section 1

The New Testament has a good deal less in the way of insane ideas, although it isn't completely devoid of them either. And in just the same way as the Old Testament, the New Testament tries to pass off what is insane as instead just being miraculous. Also, just like the Old Testament, the insanity starts right at the beginning.

> *This is how the birth of Jesus Christ came about: His mother Mary was pledged to be married to Joseph, but before they came together, she was found to be with child through the Holy Spirit. Because Joseph her husband was a righteous man and did not want to expose her to public disgrace, he had in mind to divorce her quietly.*
>
> *But after he had considered this, an angel of the Lord appeared to him in a dream and said, "Joseph son of David, do not be afraid to take Mary home as your wife, because what is conceived in her is from the Holy Spirit. She will give birth to a son, and you are to give him the name Jesus, because he will save his people from their sins."*
>
> *All this took place to fulfill what the Lord had said through the prophet: "The virgin will be with child and will give birth to a son, and they will call him Immanuel"-- which means, "God with us."*
>
> *When Joseph awoke, he did what the angel of the Lord had commanded him and took Mary home as his wife. But he had no union with her until she gave birth to a son. And he gave him the name Jesus.* - Matthew 1:18-25

So our introduction to insanity comes in the 18th verse of the very first chapter of the very first book of the New Testament. In this bit of scripture we're given the story of how a young Jewish virgin girl became impregnated by the incorporeal spirit of god known as the

Holy Ghost. She then proceeds to give birth to the son of god who is also god in human form.

The real insane thing about this is that this is where we see the line between the fundamentalist and progressive Christian start to blur. You see, both of these theological schools believe this scripture as literal truth, and because of this, there comes a point where all Christians must be literalists. No matter how progressive your views on social issues such as equality are, in order to wear the label of Christian with any degree of meaning of significance you have to acquiesce to the belief in some very insane ideas.

The real significant difference between the progressive and fundamentalist Christian, is at what point in the doctrinal narrative they begin to accept insane ideas. For the fundamentalist it starts right from the beginning. From the very first word to the last, it all must be true or else none of it is. But the progressive is more liberal, and says that much of that Old Testament stuff is just nonsense. They accept a scientific view of human origins, however there comes a point, usually starting with the New Testament, where some of this insanity has to be true, or else there's just no reason to follow at all. So, for the progressive, they must still at least believe in the virgin birth, and the other bits of insanity I will soon mention which are otherwise known as the miracles of Jesus and his disciples, in order to hold to some semblance of being a Christian at all.

So what we see here is that the progressive and fundamentalist run into the same problem, but at different points in the doctrine. We also see that you can't really call yourself a Christian if you aren't willing to make some fairly insane claims. It is one thing to claim that god is real, but it's a whole other thing to claim that he once impregnated a Jewish virgin girl. Neither of us can prove the existence or nonexistence of god, but I can surely make a valid claim that never in all of history has any physical evidence shown a virgin having given birth. The human species is rather knowledgeable about the process of reproduction, and in most species, especially with human beings, it isn't a solo act.

What makes this bit of scripture all the more perplexing, is that it's oddly reminiscent of some other stories outside the bible. If you'll recall, in a previous chapter I mentioned Nephilim and the concept of demigods. Well, here is that concept revisited. And the thing that makes this all perplexing, is that no one accepts the idea that Hercules was the son of god, and yet literally billions of people accept that Jesus was. No one honestly believes that Zeus impregnated a mortal woman and had a son, and yet the notion that Yahweh did this same thing isn't even questioned.

Now, maybe you're really thinking about this for the first time from this perspective. Maybe, you're like one of my favorite comedians Bill Burr, who talked about how this idea finally hit him in the face one day when he was making fun of how insane Scientology is and realized that he himself supposedly believed a virgin woman gave birth to a baby that could walk on water. When you finally come to think about this from this perspective, you might wonder why these ideas which are equally insane have never seemed equally insane before. The reason for this is twofold.

First of all, it's almost certain that no one ever told you that Greek or Roman mythology was factually true. When you were a child, you likely believed in Santa, the Easter bunny, and the tooth fairy, and you likely believed in them because your parents and friends and family told you they were real. But it's highly unlikely that your parents ever said, "You better behave, or Zeus will send Medusa to turn you to stone." If your parents had actually believed in that mythology as religious truth, just as the Greeks and Romans once did, you'd very likely believe it too. The reality is that most religious belief is hereditary, and that most people just believe what their parents and other family believe. Those beliefs may alter slightly over time, and may cause someone to branch off to a different sect, but at the core those born to Christian parents tend to be Christians. And the same goes for all other religions.

This inherently brings us to the next reason that many people don't see the insane nature of religious doctrine, which is that most people are indoctrinated with those ideas since they are children. The idea that a guy once walked on water and raised the dead, doesn't sound that insane when you also believe a fat man waddles his ass down the chimney once a year to bring you a kewpie doll. As you grow up, people finally tell you that the fat ass in the red suit isn't actually real, but no one says anything about the Jewish zombie who can moonwalk on water being a bit farfetched. In fact, well over a third of the adult population on this planet will tell you that Santa is hogwash in one breath, and then tell you about Jesus' supposed miracles in the next.

There's a joke that posits the notion that if you waited until your male child was old enough to understand what it was about and asked him if he wanted to be circumcised, almost no one would ever be circumcised. The same notion applies to religion in general as well. If your first introduction to religion was as a teen of 16 to 18 who had been raised to value logical thought and reason, the chances that you'd believe any of what the bible says as literal truth are slim to none... and slim just walked out the door. This is one of the reasons that all religions employ a policy of youth indoctrination. Youth programs are a very serious business for Christians, especially here in the US, because brainwashing and indoctrinating a child is far easier than doing the same to an adult. And once the seed is planted, it becomes very hard to kill that weed that starts growing there. Even attacking the roots and foundation can do little to kill that weed.

Section 2

The amount of insane ideas in the New Testament may be less, but the ideas themselves are no less insane, as you'll soon see.

Now, within the New Testament there are 37 different miracles attributed to Jesus. That doesn't include the supposed miracles performed by the apostles, nor any of the supposed miraculous revelations to the apostles and other believers. I won't consume too much of your time by going over all of these, but there are some which I'd like to touch on.

I personally prefer to separate these miracles into two classifications. First, we have what I consider parlor tricks, such as the water into wine trick. These are miracles which while highly improbable, are still within the range of physical possibility. They are acts which others have recreated through sleight of hand or other illusory techniques. Then we have what are physical impossibilities, such as raising people from the dead. These are acts which no amount of trickery can reproduce, because they require someone to break the laws of nature rather than bending them or tricking the mind into believing they occurred.

I'll discuss a few of the parlor tricks first.

> *On the third day a wedding took place at Cana in Galilee. Jesus' mother was there, and Jesus and his disciples had also been invited to the wedding. When the wine was gone, Jesus' mother said to him, "They have no more wine."*
>
> *"Woman, why do you involve me?" Jesus replied. "My hour has not yet come."*
>
> *His mother said to the servants, "Do whatever he tells you."*
>
> *Nearby stood six stone water jars, the kind used by the Jews for ceremonial washing, each holding from twenty to*

thirty gallons.

Jesus said to the servants, "Fill the jars with water"; so they filled them to the brim.

Then he told them, "Now draw some out and take it to the master of the banquet."

They did so, and the master of the banquet tasted the water that had been turned into wine. He did not realize where it had come from, though the servants who had drawn the water knew. Then he called the bridegroom aside and said, "Everyone brings out the choice wine first and then the cheaper wine after the guests have had too much to drink; but you have saved the best till now."

What Jesus did here in Cana of Galilee was the first of the signs through which he revealed his glory; and his disciples believed in him. - John 2:1-11

Now, one of the things you'll see me continue to talk about is the reliability of source information. The reason for this is that, the validity of a claim can only be determined by the reliability of the source material and the physical evidence to support the claim. And the problem we run into with the bible is that in all instances every bit of the source material is second or third hand hearsay. Quite often in fact, what we have are oral accounts of events that supposedly happened which have been passed along by word of mouth for generations. What makes this issue even worse is the fact that there is absolutely no physical evidence to support these claims.

Before we simply accept this story as fact, we need to ask ourselves a few questions. The first of them being, is this act physically possible by natural means? The answer to that question is a resounding no. There is no natural physical means by which to turn water into wine. In every case where wine is made, it is a process of rendering the juice from grapes and fermenting those juices. That is the only way to make wine. But of course, this lack of natural physical explanation is why this is labeled as a miracle.

The next two questions we must ask are complimentary. First, we must ask if the source of this information is reliable, and then if there is any physical evidence to substantiate the claim.

As to the first question, although this book is attributed to the apostle John, he isn't the actual author. The fact is, that we don't know who the author is at all. Furthermore, we don't even know for a fact that the apostle John even existed at all. Outside of the bible, there is actually zero evidence of this man's existence at all. So the author of this story could have been anyone from a delusional drunkard to a saintly acolyte of the cult of Christ. The veracity of this claim then, gets no support from the author because we don't know who the author is and so we have no valid reason to simply accept their word as to this claim or any other.

This is where physical evidence becomes so very important. You see, because we cannot validate the claim based on the merits of the claimant alone, we must try to substantiate the claim with observable physical evidence. So, if we are unable to claim truth to this claim by means of a trusted source, and there is no physical evidence to support the claim, which are both true in this case, we have no valid reason to believe the claim.

A good analogy for this would be, if someone were to claim that I could fly. If someone were to make such a claim, we would ask for validation of such a claim with physical evidence. If no such evidence exists, then we should not simply accept the claim, even if the claim is a firsthand account and even if we trust the person making said claim.

This is where the idea of faith comes back into play, and where the Christian will claim that these authors of the bible were inspired by god and so they claim that the authors can be trusted. The fallacious nature of this argument becomes apparent when we look at the fact that all throughout history men have made this very same claim to being inspired by god. The crusades and inquisitions were also said to be inspired by god. Muhammad claimed to be inspired by god. Jim Jones claimed to be inspired by god. Hell, even George W Bush claimed to be inspired by god when he invaded Iraq. So this claim falls short of being a valid reason for trust or belief, and the claim itself is only supported by the claimant having made the claim in the first place, or someone making the claim on another's behalf.

So the reality of the situation becomes that you have one claim that is only supported by another claim, and not a bit of it has any valid physical evidence to substantiate it. If you're going to accept that as valid proof of something, then you may as well also believe that I can fly. I mean, all I need to do is claim that I can fly and that I was inspired by god to be able to fly, and whether or not you've seen me fly you should still just accept it on faith because I made the claim in the name of god.

Does that sound reasonable to you?

Now, before we move on, there's one more thing I want you to look at with this story. As interesting as this supposed miracle is, the thing which is more interesting, at least to me, is that we see in this story that Jesus actually breaks one of the Ten Commandments. If you look at this story, Jesus actually gets very rude with his own mother. One might even say he gets downright petulant. His basic statement is, "Who the hell are you to bother me with your nonsense woman". Now, what people often fail to consider is the fact that Jesus was a Jew, and as such he was obligated to follow Jewish law. One of those laws is to honor thy mother and father, but here we see Jesus flat out disrespecting his mother like she's just some common slave girl.

If you're familiar with Jewish law, the punishment for a disobedient child was to drag them into the street and stone them to death. So not only does Jesus break a commandment, but every person at this wedding feast also violates Jewish law by not stoning Jesus to death on the spot for his disregard of Jewish law. Of course, since Jesus claimed to be the son of god special pleading can be applied to say that Jesus has no obligation to follow these commandments.

Section 3

Now, I want to skip ahead a good bit to three major miracles, and will return to all the rest briefly after that. The three major miracles I want to discuss are actually the same supposed miracle performed on three different occasions, which is the supposed miracle of Jesus raising people from the dead.

These are listed in the book of Luke 7:11-17 when Jesus raises a widow's son from the dead, the occasion of Jesus raising Jairus' daughter from the dead as listed in Matthew 9:18, Mark 5:21-24, and Luke 8:40-42, and lastly, the most notable occasion when Jesus raises Lazarus from the dead as offered in John 11:1-45. These events supposedly take place in slightly different ways under different circumstances, however they all have one thing in common which is that they are an act which is by all reasonable measure of reality a physical impossibility.

Now, the first thing I want us to understand is what death truly is. A lot of people mistake nearly dead with dead all the time. We may talk about someone who went into cardiac arrest as having died, or someone that went into pulmonary arrest and stopped breathing as having died. But the reality is that those people didn't actually die. They just came real close to it. So when we talk about death we have to understand that there is a definitive diagnosis for what actually constitutes death. Death is when the brain can no longer sustain the functions of your body. In technical terms this is called brain death, because once the brain fails everything else fails with it.

The reason that understanding this is so important, is that we haven't always understood this, and even if we had we couldn't detect it until rather recently in our history. Although mankind has been studying the brain for some great many generations, our knowledge has progressed in baby steps. Neuroscience is still a very young discipline, and yet, the amount of insight we've gained already from this field has completely transformed our understanding of the human mind at its most fundamental levels.

So what we must understand is that when the brain dies it is true death. There is almost no coming back from that. The reason I say almost is that, in the modern age there have been some extremely rare cases where someone has been declared brain dead and their brains have begun functioning again. Now, when I say rare I don't mean like hitting the lottery rare. Your chances of hitting the lottery are about 1 in 2 million, however your chances of coming back from brain death are about 1 in 7.1 billion. And, we must also realize that without the aid of machines to keep your body alive until your brain starts to function again, your chances of survival are nil.

The whole reason I want us to understand this, is because as we proceed I'm going to tell you that there are three explanations for these accounts, as well as all of Jesus' other supposed miracles. Two of these explanations are completely logical and rational. One of them however, is absolutely illogical and irrational, and by no coincidence at all this last irrational explanation is the one most generally given and accepted by Christians.

The first rational answer, which ties back into what I've been talking about with brain death, is the notion that witnesses simply made a mistake. Without proper knowledge in any given situation human beings are prone to making mistakes. Our tactile senses such as sight, smell, taste, and touch, are only marginally reliable and are often easily confused. You can easily tell the difference between cotton and leather while blindfolded, but try telling the difference between real leather and faux leather while blindfolded. It isn't very easy, and most of us couldn't do it. The same can be said about our vision. We are often easily tricked or distracted when it comes to what we think we see. I've heard it said that you should only trust 75% of what you see and 50% of what you hear, but I think those numbers are a bit generous.

So if we are going to allow for the notion that someone did actually see something, we must acknowledge that those people may have been totally wrong, or confused, about what they saw. Since we can't speak to the eyewitnesses and see if we have multiple matching accounts of these events, we must admit that this isn't a reliable source. Also, we have no outside corroborating evidence to support the claim. It is one thing when your friends tell a story about you, but when strangers or your enemy tell the same story it adds a great measure of validity to your story. Unfortunately for Christianity, there is a marked lack of independent corroboration for the accounts in the bible. There are no contemporary accounts of any figure from the bible including Jesus himself. The earliest accounts come some forty years after Jesus was supposedly crucified, and even then are second or third hand accounts.

The second reasonable and logical conclusion is that people just made things up or exaggerated these things in order to lionize this character Jesus. It is very common for people to exaggerate or even invent claims for those who they want to paint a portrait of exceptionalism for. Often times the most extraordinary stories are born from simple truths that grow into massive falsehoods. Perhaps Jesus showed up at a wedding which ran out of wine and he just happened to have more in his caravan. Perhaps he showed up at someone's home and their child was in a comatose state and happened to come out of that state while Jesus happened to be there. Such simple acts could grow into massive tales almost overnight.

The third explanation, which is wholly irrational and illogical, is to believe that Jesus could perform supernatural feats of magic. This tends to be the go-to explanation for most Christians. Of course

Jesus could perform acts of magic if he was the son of god. This seems like a semi logical statement, until we dig a little deeper. Now, the reason this becomes illogical is that, if we examine the bible we see a curious thing, which is that Satan actually has diminutive power over humans. In particular we must look at the ideas of demon possession and witchcraft as being the main tools used by Satan to influence and manipulate mankind. These too are supernatural events that carry with them the weight of magical powers. If one is going to believe in Jesus having magical powers, then they must also acquiesce to the notion of demonic and dark supernatural forces being just as real and just as plausible. But since the advent of photography and videography, recording and experimentation, there has been not one shred of real physical evidence of any form of supernatural magic.

I want you to ask yourself why, if witchcraft and demonic magic and power were real, aren't there witches running around in control of everything? Why, if these things are real, do we not live in a world like that of the television show Supernatural? If these things were real, and let us not forget that the bible and Jesus himself both claim they are real, they should be so abundant and noticeable that they could not be ignored or disputed. But even with 7 billion people on this planet, the few events that people do say they've experienced that are of an unexplainable paranormal nature are so rare and few, that there is still no physical evidence that they ever even took place. You can live to be 1,000 years old and I promise you that you'll never meet an actual witch that can manipulate matter and space and time via magic. If people could wield such power they would be nearly unstoppable.

Section 4

I could sit here and go over all the rest of these supposed miracles, and explain to you why these things are physically impossible and why there's no valid reason to believe in them, but what would be the point? If you haven't gotten the message by now, then you probably aren't going to. So instead of going into all that I want to talk about the two most insane aspects of the New Testament. Not because I think they'll sway anyone that hasn't already been swayed, but because they truly highlight the level of insanity one must acquiesce to even when leaving all the Old Testament nonsense behind.

The first bit of insanity I want to talk about is the apostle Paul. Now, the thing which makes Paul himself the architect of insanity is the fact that 13 of 27 books in the New Testament are attributed to him. This number is greater than any other supposed biblical author, although we must keep in mind that even these books of the bible attributed to the apostle Paul are not first-hand accounts. They are copies of copies written mostly from an oral record. The thing which makes this insane is not the amount of content attributed to this man but rather, the fact that he never actually met Jesus as a living man. Paul's only claim to knowledge of Jesus was through a supposed meeting between Paul and the ghost of Jesus. In fact, before this meeting Paul was actually known as Saul of Tarsus and supposedly actively participated in the persecution of the early cult following of Jesus and its followers.

Yet, for all intents and purposes, this man Paul almost singlehandedly builds the Christian faith and the early Christian church. The codes of conduct governing Christianity all come from the Pauline letters to the churches at Corinth, Ephesus, Rome, and to the Colossians. So this man, who by his own supposed admission never even met Jesus, supposedly authors nearly half of the New Testament, including the prescriptions for daily life as a

Christian, and is seen as the ultimate authority of the word of Jesus. Not Peter who supposedly walked side by side with Jesus. Not Thomas or Mark or Luke who supposedly stood side by side with Jesus at the Sermon on the Mount. This man Paul, heretic turned saint, is seen as the authoritative word on all things Jesus.

What makes this even worse is that Paul often seems to contradict not only the other apostles, but even Jesus himself. It is Paul who poses the pro-Roman atmosphere of the New Testament and this sort of underlying anti-Semitic feel of that half of the bible. It is Paul's embrace of apocalypticism that leads to the heavy weight given to matters such as chastity and sexual purity. It is Paul who reiterates the prescription for death to homosexuals as offered in Leviticus. It is Paul whose misogyny shines through within the New Testament, while Jesus himself could be said to be a champion of women and an idealist in his day when it came to ideas of equality between the sexes. Jesus, who supposedly treated the common harlot Mary of Magdalene as a saint, would seem to be at odds with Paul's very anti-female stance offered by the Pauline letters.

By all rights, the man whose most credited with authorship of the vast majority of the New Testament, only has authority by making the claim that he talked to a ghost once. This is an absolutely absurd and preposterous idea to accept in the same way it is absurd to believe that the so called prophet Muhammad rode to heaven on the back of a Pegasus as the Qur'an and Hadith claim. It is just as absurd and insane as the man who claims that the neighbor's dog spoke to him and told him to murder his family. Whether it's talking to ghosts, flying horses, or a talking dog, it's all absurd and it's all insane.

Lastly in regards to the New Testament, we have quite possibly the most insane book of the entire bible which is the book of Revelation. If you only read one book of the bible, this is the one I recommend. Supposedly given through a divine dream to a man named John who lived on the island of Patmos, this book tells of the supposed coming apocalypse. It features famine, plagues, demons, a dragon, and a whole smorgasbord of other absolutely insane magical and supernatural ideas. This is the book that the idea of the rapture comes from as well as the notion of the Antichrist who is supposedly a satanic version of Jesus. This book takes all the other insanity of the bible, turns it up to 11, rips the knob off and plugs it into another amplifier just in case it wasn't loud enough to begin with.

However, if there is one chapter or group of passages from this book of the bible which stands as the most insane idea of all, it is this passage right at the very end:

> *"I am Alpha and Omega, the beginning and the end, the first and the last.*

> *Blessed are they that do his commandments, that they may have right to the tree of life, and may enter in through the gates into the city.*

> *For without are dogs, and sorcerers, and whoremongers, and murderers, and idolaters, and whosoever loveth and maketh a lie.*

> *I Jesus have sent mine angel to testify unto you these things in the churches. I am the root and the offspring of David, and the bright and morning star.*

> *And the Spirit and the bride say, Come. And let him that heareth say, Come. And let him that is athirst come. And whosoever will, let him take the water of life freely.*

For I testify unto every man that heareth the words of the prophecy of this book, If any man shall add unto these things, God shall add unto him the plagues that are written in this book:

And if any man shall take away from the words of the book of this prophecy, God shall take away his part out of the book of life, and out of the holy city, and from the things which are written in this book.

He which testifieth these things saith, Surely I come quickly. Amen. Even so, come, Lord Jesus.

The grace of our Lord Jesus Christ be with you all. Amen."
- Revelation 22:13-21

The basic idea of this passage is this; every bit of this story is completely factual and anyone who believes this will get a cookie from Jesus himself, but if you don't believe it you try to change it some way, then god is going to torture you mercilessly... in Jesus' name, amen.

It doesn't matter how insane these ideas are, you're just supposed to believe them because some guy said he talked to god once. It doesn't matter if you know that dragons aren't real and that donkeys and snakes can't talk. You still have to believe it or face the potential eternal punishment of this vengeful god. There is no better quote in all the bible to substantiate the notion that Christianity is truly an all or nothing proposal than this last few lines of the bible. It shows very clearly that you either believe in these insane ideas or you simply aren't a Christian by any theological standards.

Chapter 4 :

Fundamentalism
By
Proxy

Section 1

The line between fundamentalism and progressive religious belief, seems at first glance to be fairly cut and dry. After all, it's easy to tell a progressive Christian from a fundie any day of the week. That line is most definitely noticeable when we look at social issues such as gay marriage and abortion and several other social issues. But that line isn't nearly as clear as most of us think it is, and for good reason.

You see, as we've explored these insane ideas we've come to see that on both sides of that line, people acquiesce to many of these ideas in a very literal sense. The progressive may agree that the genesis myth or the ark is fiction, and yet still offer that the supposed miracles of Jesus are factually true. So when we get down to the heart of the matter, this line is really just one of semantics. It's simply a matter of at what point and to what degree one is willing to accept insanity as a valid factual statement. The absolute truth is that, there is nothing any more or less insane about believing that Jesus resurrected people from death, than it is to believe that Abraham received divine guidance from a burning bush that could talk. These are equally insane ideas, and regardless of how progressive one's personal views on social issues are, they still have to accept some very insane ideas in order to wear the label of Christian.

Now, this is where the idea of fundamentalism by proxy comes in, because you need the fundamental beginnings of the doctrine in order to support the ideas which follow after. You need Adam and Eve to get to Noah, and Noah to get to Abraham, and Abraham to get to Moses, and so on and so forth all the way up to Jesus. If even one of the links in this chain fails, then it will not truly hold. You can piecemeal the whole thing together with flimsy bits of philosophical thread, but such threads can easily be pulled and cause the whole thing to unravel.

So the progressive becomes a fundamentalist by proxy, by the very necessity of a chain of events. This necessity is what allows fundamentalism to exist at all, because it isn't as if the progressive can simply dismiss the Old Testament and still postulate a need for Jesus as savior. By accepting that the Old Testament is necessary to get to the New Testament and to provide a validation for the need of Jesus as savior, the progressive offers a measure of validity to the fundamentalist position. This means that the progressive needs these fundamental beginnings to validate their position, while the fundamentalist has no reason to accept a more progressive worldview because they are simply taking the doctrine at its word. So the progressive needs the fundamentalist perspective, but the fundamentalist has no real need for the progressive perspective, and can dismiss it entirely.

The cold hard fact, is that without the fundamental tales of the bible all the way back to the book of Genesis, Christianity makes about as much sense as a petroleum jelly biscuit. Sure it's jelly... but no one wants to eat that. And what is worse is that fundamentalists like Ken Ham and Ray Comfort and the like, know this all too well. That's why men like Comfort will tell you that if you aren't following a literal interpretation of the bible, that you aren't really a Christian. As much as I hate to say it, Comfort is absolutely correct about this, and for all the same reasons I've been pointing out in this book. If you reject the Genesis myth, then you reject the necessity of Jesus altogether. If you think a burning bush that could talk is a load of dingo's kidneys, then you reject the foundation of the establishment of Judaism and in so doing reject the notion of Christ's authority as king of the Jews.

I'm sorry folks, but that's really just how it works. It's like a Jenga tower that is so precariously stacked that to remove even one block will surely cause it to topple.

Section 2

So maybe you're beginning to see the real problem at hand. You see, no matter which side of the fundamentalist versus progressive line you stand, you're still agreeing with some very insane ideas, and even the progressive offers vindication for fundamentalist nonsense by offering that the ideas which are built on fundamental doctrine that lead to the necessity of Jesus as savior are at least to some degree valid. There simply is no logical and rational basis for the belief in Jesus as the savior of mankind without all the nonsense that supposedly leads to that presumed necessity. All the progressive is doing is to cherry pick the parts they like while trying to ignore all the rest. But you just can't do that and still try to pose a reasonable argument in favor of Christianity.

Despite what people want to believe, Christianity, like nearly all other religions, is an all or nothing proposition. Either you accept it as truth, or you're just playing at it and pretending to be a Christian. And the reality of what the bible teaches is that, if there is a heaven and a hell, the ones who'll go to heaven are these fundamentalist wankers, rather than those who instead of blindly following the bible have chosen to make a conscious decision about their position and worldview based on a more realistic perspective. If what the bible teaches were true, then heaven probably isn't a place that most of us would enjoy even if we could get in.

So let's get down to the nitty gritty here. If you can't accept the bible as truth from front to back, then you really don't accept Jesus and you really aren't a Christian. But, I'm here to tell you that this is the best news you'll hear today. You've likely only ever worn the label of Christian out of tradition and custom, and you've likely never given any thoughts to just how insane the doctrine of Christianity truly is. And if you aren't willing to accept that insanity then there is an easy solution...

Just let it go.

Section 3

Actor and comedian Bill Burr once talked about this very idea in one of his comedy specials titled I'm Sorry You Feel That Way. In this special, Burr talks about coming to the realization that there was no real difference between the insane ideas of Christianity and those of any other religion. In coming to that realization, he said he had to ask himself what he was going to do about this 800lb gorilla of religion that he was carrying on his back. He could either cling persistently to those insane ideas, becoming one of those people who claim offense at any criticism of this nonsense, or he could be one of those progressive types who doesn't really go to church or even actual believe these things who only wears the label of Christian out of tradition or social convention, or lastly, he could just let it all go. In the end he chose option three, and to just let it go. He likened this to the sport of curling in one of the best analogies I've ever heard. He said that it was like being the shooter in a curling event who lines up with the rock at the shooting line and takes a few steps to build forward momentum. The shooter holds the rock and begins sliding down the narrow strip of ice towards the points section of the curling surface. When you see this, you tend to think that the shooter is in it for the long haul and is going to travel down the ice with the rock. But at a certain point the shooter simply releases the rock, stands up, and just slowly backs away to let the rock travel its course.

Here's the rub though; letting go of your religion has consequences. Chiefly, this action carries with it the consequence of potentially losing some, or even all, of your friends and even your family. There's no way for me to sugarcoat that, and I won't lie to you and act as if it won't happen. The flat out truth is that, the vast majority of people who let go of their religion end up losing friends and family over that decision. And it isn't just those who let go of their religion and decide to wear the label of atheist who endure this shunning. Even if you simply call yourself agnostic, or if you subscribe to deism or some sort of spirituality, you're very likely to be shunned by those who still hold to their religious beliefs.

So the question you have to ask yourself is, is it worth it?

I had to ask myself that question before I came out as an atheist. I knew what the consequences could be, and I had to ask myself if being honest about who I am and how I truly feel, was worth losing people that I truly care about. The fact is, making that decision was one of the hardest decisions I've ever faced. In the end, I just couldn't handle the idea of letting religion make me a liar. I couldn't accept lying to everyone about who I am and how I truly feel. Most of all, I couldn't keep lying to myself, because doing so was such a mental and physical drain on me as an individual. So, I chose my integrity over simply maintaining what was comforting and familiar. I chose to be true to myself above all else.

But make no mistake; this wasn't the correct answer, because there is no set in stone correct answer. Each of us must make our own decision based on our own understanding and our own ideals as to what we value more. Some people will continue to fake it and go through the motions, even though they don't actually believe in these insane ideas, simply to hold on to the friends and family that they value. And while I can't tell anyone that this is wrong per se, I can tell you that it is completely dishonest. Now, maybe you can live with that dishonesty, but I just couldn't, and for many other atheists and non-religious people the same is true. Many of us just couldn't keep lying and faking it. It just isn't worth it to us to live a lie for the sake of false comfort.

I know that this sounds like a very selfish position to take. It may seem as though this position is insensitive to our friends and families, but honestly it isn't. We often act as though there are lies which are acceptable, and we see them as being acceptable because we believe that the truth will hurt those around us. And maybe if we can manage to keep that lie to ourselves, then we spare others the pain of having to deal with the truth, but most of the time we fail miserably at this. The truth almost always comes out because our lies have a way of growing. We tell one little lie, and then we have to tell another little lie to keep that first lie hidden and on a long enough timeline this can often just snowball out of hand and become this horrible monster of a thing that we have to fight with every day just to keep it contained. If any of these lies ever come to the surface, then we've now betrayed the trust of those around us that we thought we were protecting.

One of the greatest acts of kindness we can show those whom we care about, is to always offer them honesty. Even if being honest will cause strife; even if it may cost us a relationship, if we truly respect those we claim to care about, we owe them our honesty. Even if they hate us for it, they deserve the respect of our honesty. And what's more is that, we should respect ourselves enough to always bring honesty to the table, no matter how hard that may be or what the consequences may be, we owe that to ourselves.

I myself am very lucky, because although I did lose a great many friends for my honesty, my family has for the most part come to accept my position and the fact that I'm just trying to be honest. They don't agree with it, and they don't like it, but they accept it and they respect my honesty. And really, that's what we have to hope for when we make such a decision to be forthright about these things. We have to hope, that they can understand and accept us for who we are. As harsh as it may sound, if they can't accept our honesty that is a problem that we can't fix because it's their problem rather than ours and the only person whom you have true control over on this planet is yourself. You can't force them to accept anything. All you can do is to be honest and hope for the best.

Section 4

One of the things that many religious people try to use to bolster their position, is the notion that no one can prove that god doesn't exist. Now, while I could attack this premise on the simple fact that it is a fallacious argument which seeks to negate the burden of proof, I'd much rather explain why it simply isn't factually true. Or, more accurately, it's only a half-truth.

You see, while it is factually true that no one can prove that there is absolutely no god at all, that doesn't mean that one cannot factually prove that a specific god of a given religion does not exist. The fact of the matter is that, each and every religion gives a fairly specific account of their god or gods through their various doctrines. The bible gives very specific accounts of the supposed acts which the Christian and Jewish god supposedly engaged in. From Genesis to Revelation, the bible is meant to be a factual account of that particular god's supposed interactions with mankind. So when we weigh these accounts against known factual information such as we are given by scientific disciplines including geology, archaeology, physics, biology, and even cosmology, what we run into is an absolute contradiction between what can be factually proven by science and the claims which are made in the doctrine of the bible. This very clear and abundant contradiction leads to the inevitable conclusion that only one of these two opposing positions can be valid, and if we are honest with ourselves we must admit that only one of these positions has any verifiable substance. Of these two opposing positions, the bible is based entirely off of hearsay, while the scientific position has such an abundance of factual and observable evidence to support it, that to deny that evidence is in itself an act of embracing insanity.

This is exactly why men such as Ken Ham and Ray Comfort and many others, tell their followers that one must first believe the bible, no matter how insane those ideas are, and then refuse to believe anything which contradicts the bible, no matter how much supporting evidence those contradictory statements made by science have to substantiate them. This is a lot like a judge instructing jurors that the defendant is already guilty based entirely on the fact that the judge says he's guilty and asking the jury to overlook all evidence to the contrary. This is a completely biased position based solely on an unsubstantiated claim of authority, which asks of the believer to disregard all objections no matter how valid those objections truly are.

So, even if the bible were not full to bursting with insane ideas, philosophical paradoxes, and self-contradictory statements, which it most certainly is, we would still be entirely justified in dismissing the fundamentalist position based solely on the fact that the only way that it makes any sense at all is from an entirely biased starting point. There is absolutely no way that such a position can be even the least bit objective, and so that position should not be trusted in the least. The flat out fact is that, if you can't validate your position from an objective standpoint with factual evidence, then you don't have a valid position at all. And of course, once we dismiss the fundamentalist position, we may as well just dismiss the whole of Christianity as being an invalid, illogical, irrational, and insane proposition.

The thing I want to stress most here however, is that without progressive Christians as the smiling face of Christianity, fundamentalism hasn't got a leg to stand on. And without fundamentalism and the foundational doctrinal insanity, progressives are just playing at being Christians. It is this inherent symbiotic relationship that makes the most aggressive sorts of fundamentalism, such as what we see from the Westboro Baptist church and even the KKK, even a possibility. If they did not have progressives to point at and claim that the fundamentalist position is just a differing viewpoint of Christianity, everyone would have to admit without reservation that these fundamentalists are nothing more than hatemongers, and that these groups are nothing more than hate groups hiding behind religion.

Chapter 5 :

Ten Questions Biblical Literalists Cannot Honestly Answer

There are certain questions that no biblical literalist can answer honestly. This isn't to say that they can't answer these questions at all, but only that any answer they give is either an evasion of actually answering the question, or the answer is absolutely fallacious. So here are ten questions that no biblical literalist can answer honestly. There are many other questions like this that will trip up any biblical literalist, but these are some of my favorites.

PART ONE

1. Can you make a moral judgment against rape or slavery using only scripture?

The position of biblical literalism can really make justifying your position on issues like rape and slavery very difficult. Most every Christian I know, whether a progressive or fundamentalist and literalist, will tell you that rape and slavery are unethical and morally wrong. The progressive Christian who has embraced a secular worldview, has that secular and logical worldview to fall back on to justify their moral judgment. The literalist however, does not have this luxury.

So when the literalist is taken to task on this and asked to justify his moral judgment based on a strictly biblical worldview, they run into a problem. The problem they run into is that there is absolutely zero scripture that says these acts are acts of moral turpitude. They can search the bible till their fingers fly off, and not once will find a single scripture that says rape and slavery are morally wrong.

Not even one.

The bible does address these issues, however the issues are addressed as property issues.

For the part of rape, there is a guideline for what to do if someone rapes your virgin daughter. This issue is addressed from the perspective that one's daughter is one's property and that the act of rape diminishes the value of that property. Apparently, to make amends for the damage of that man's property, the rapist is to marry the girl whom he attacked and violated and give her dad some money. [2] Nowhere in this scripture is there any mention that the act of rape itself is a morally reprehensible act.

Now, maybe you're thinking that this only addresses what to do if your daughter gets raped, but what if your son gets raped? Well, oddly enough, the punishment for a man raping another man's son would be death. The odd thing about this however, is not that the punishment is more severe for a man who rapes a boy than one who rapes a girl, but rather why it is more severe. You see a man who rapes a boy would be committing a homosexual act, and homosexual acts actually are labeled as an act of moral turpitude. So the man would not be put to death for the act of rape, but rather for engaging in a homosexual act. Furthermore, this applied to all homosexual acts and not just a homosexual rape incident.

As for the issue of slavery, there's actually a good bit of scripture on the subject. Yet none of that scripture addresses this as a moral issue. Instead, the scriptures offer a framework for how to be a good and obedient slave, and how a slave owner should treat their slaves at least as well as they treat the rest of their property. Once again however, we see that nowhere in the scriptures does it actually say that slavery is morally reprehensible.

This question is actually one of my favorites because it addresses a very serious flaw on the literalist's part, in an argument that has been raging for years. For quite some time Christians of all stripes, but especially the literalist crowd, have argued that atheists and secularists lack an objective basis for moral judgment. And also that, secular ethics are just something stolen from the Christian worldview. Yet, with this one question and the implications of its honest answer, their argument is shown to be entirely without merit. In fact, I argue that secular ethics, rooted in a logical evaluation of moral issues, is the only objective basis for moral judgment, and that it is far superior to a literal biblical worldview.

My secular ethical position and worldview says implicitly that rape and slavery are morally reprehensible and unethical acts. Furthermore, my worldview can back up that assertion from a strictly objective logical stance. And most importantly, any Christian who wishes to justify a moral judgment against these acts, must actually acquiesce to a secular ethical reasoning to do so. Any literalist who makes a moral judgment against these things, has no biblical justification for that judgment and so they too are employing secular ethics which makes them a hypocrite.

2. Would you sacrifice your child if god asked you to?

Most of us have heard this question. If you're an atheist who enjoys debate and engaging theists in rational discourse, you've likely asked this question. The most common answer given by any theist at all, is that their god wouldn't ever ask them to do that. They will tell you that their god is a kind and loving god who wouldn't ask someone to murder their own child as a sacrifice. And to that I must say, "Then you don't believe in the god of the bible".

This question was posed to evangelical fundamentalist minister and liar for Jesus, Ray Comfort on his Facebook page once, and his response was one of the first honest ones I've ever seen. Granted, he had to be backed into a corner to give that honest answer. After trying to deflect and dodge the question, Comfort finally broke and lashed out saying that yes, he would indeed murder his children if god asked him to. He'd like you to believe that this is a testament to his unwavering faith, however I'm somewhat certain that it is actually just a sign of how deeply rooted his insanity truly is.

The reason that this was the only honest answer that Comfort could give, is because anything else would negate his claim to biblical literalism and inerrancy. You see, despite what many Christians want to believe, the bible makes it very clear that god has, and therefore could again, ask for someone to murder their own child as a sacrifice. Christians will point to the scripture of Abraham's near murder and sacrifice of Isaac and say, "See. God stayed his hand which shows that god would never ask me to do that". Of course, they overlook the other bits of scripture where god actually did allow a child sacrifice. They also conveniently overlook the fact that god supposedly sacrificed his own son to himself on humanity's behalf.

So if we simply look at the scripture, we can see by god's supposed past track record that this is something he has done before, and so it isn't outside the realm of possibility. Now, as a biblical literalist and minister, Ray Comfort understood this logic, and gave the biblically justifiable answer. The real problem is that Ray sees nothing at all wrong with this. He is fully committed to a path of pure insanity and is happily walking along like it's a Sunday stroll through a beautiful meadow. And to show just how insane old Ray is, I'd like to point out that Ray has on more than one occasion condemned the acts of people who say they were spoken to by god or angels or demons. He has embraced the notion that those people are insane, and yet still holds to the idea that if he thought god was talking to him, that wouldn't be insane.

Of course god would talk to Ray Comfort! But Jesus telling a woman to murder and eat her own baby... Why that's just insane.

3. Is it acceptable to cherry pick the bible and only follow the parts you agree with?

Okay, this is actually a trick question. The reality is that nearly everyone, from every denomination of Christianity, cherry picks the bible. Literalists like Comfort and Ham will tell you that homosexuality is a morally reprehensible act and an abomination unto the lord, and will point to the bible as justification for their own bigotry. Of course, when you point out that it also says to stone your unruly child to death and not to eat bacon wrapped shrimp, well suddenly those parts don't apply to them.

The reason this is a trick question is because biblical literalists almost always say that cherry picking is a big no-no. So this question brings to light their absolute hypocrisy. They say all sorts of things, and yet when it's all said and done they don't actually live up to most of what they claim to believe.

Of course, if you live in any civilized society, you actually can't follow the bible literally. Let me rephrase that. You **can** follow the bible literally, but you'll end up dead or in prison. In civilized societies the notion of murdering your child for disobedience seems barbaric. Of course, barbaric is a nice way to put it because in all actuality that idea is just flat out insane. And it doesn't really matter why someone does it either. Whether you think god talks to you or you think god talked to someone else in the past and so you follow the book written by a third party that tells their story, it's all really equally insane.

4. How did animal X get from point Y to point Z after the great flood?

This may seem like a weird question, but it just takes some understanding of the variables at play here.

You see, animal X can be any number of animals. From kangaroos and Tasmanian devils, to any number of other regionally specific animal such as my favorite, the penguin.

Point Y is actually not a variable, but is actually a set location. That location being ancient Mesopotamia.

And finally, point Z is any variable geographic location.

So, this question could be worded like this:

"How did penguins get from ancient Mesopotamia to Antarctica?"

Or

"How did kangaroos get from ancient Mesopotamia to Australia?"

Now, I'll go ahead and spoil the fun here, and tell you that there is not one single word in the bible about how this happened. The bible claims that two of every animal, a male and female, got onto the boat. We assume they got off the boat at the same spot the boat landed where Noah and his family got off. That would be a mountain in the Arab region of the world. So how did penguins get from there to Antarctica? And how did kangaroos get to Australia?

The bible has nothing to say on the matter. But science, on the other hand, has a lot to say about it.

First off, science tells us that it is nearly a physical impossibility for one male and one female to preserve a species. Especially a species who often only produces one or two offspring in a lifetime. If infant mortality doesn't wipe them out, genetic disorders due to inbreeding almost certainly would.

But let's assume that they live and mate and repopulate. They certainly can't do this in a state of persistent migration. So it seems that there would need to be at least some period of repopulation before migration. If that's the case, there should be evidence of this. But I can promise you that no one is ever going to dig up penguin or kangaroo remains in Baghdad. The reason no one will ever dig up remains of those animals in the Arab region is because those animals have never lived in that region of this planet. In fact, penguins have never existed anywhere above the equator other than the Galapagos Islands.

Penguins and kangaroos and a whole laundry list of other regionally specific species, did not migrate from a mountain in the ancient Arabian region to their current location. Even if the bible said they did, which it doesn't, it still would be an utterly insane proposition to put forward.

5. How did carnivorous dinosaurs supposedly eat plants before the biblical fall of man, when their teeth and digestive systems were not equipped to process a vegetarian diet?

Ken Ham and Ray Comfort, as well as many other biblical literalists, have made the claim before that dinosaurs used to all be herbivores. Furthermore, they'd have us believe that men and dinosaurs lived side by side. Apparently the velociraptor was really a fun loving dude who's just misunderstood.

The most insane part of this proposition is actually not the assertion itself, but that it's actually saner than the assertions of other literalists in the past. There once was a time when many biblical literalists claimed that dinosaur fossils were put on earth by Satan in order to trick men into not believing in god. I think we would all agree that the vegetarian Flintstones idea is a slight improvement over the conspiracy theory involving a cosmic demon lord. Not a huge improvement mind you, but an improvement nonetheless.

Of course, this herbivore dinosaur idea is still a rather insane idea and the bible doesn't say anything at all about it either. In fact, the bible doesn't say anything at all about dinosaurs. It mentions a unicorn, a talking snake, a talking donkey, a talking bush that was eternally engulfed in flames, and a dragon, but not one mention of dinosaurs. Even if it did, it still wouldn't explain how animals with carnivorous teeth and digestive systems could subsist on plant matter.

6. Can god tell a lie?

This is a variation of the old can god make a rock so heavy that he can't lift question. The major difference here is that I address the issue from a strictly philosophical standpoint without invoking the science of physics. I find this to be a more appealing route, because religion is all about philosophy. So my tact has always been to fight bad philosophy with good philosophical arguments.

So what we have with this question is a classic paradox situation. If god is omnipotent then god can do anything including lying. However, the bible says that god is the epitome of goodness and that lying is an act of moral turpitude. So no being which is wholly good could possibly also be a liar, and yet any being which cannot lie cannot also be omnipotent, because being incapable of lying would be a limitation that no omnipotent being should be beholden too.

Another very good variation of this question, is to pose the paradox of omniscience versus free will. In that form, the question becomes whether or not man can have free will while god simultaneously has omniscience. The paradox there lies in the idea that if god is omniscient and can honestly know exactly what will happen in the future, then mankind can't have free will. And if mankind has true free will, then god can't be omniscient.

The reason for this paradox is very simple. You see, if you have true free will, then god can't know for sure what you will do until you choose to do it. And if god is omniscient, then he knows every choice you're going to make even before you make it and there can be no choice to stray from that path. So we see that the two ideas, just like god being benevolent and omnipotent, are mutually exclusive to one another.

These sorts of philosophical paradoxes are the bane of most literalists who debate these issues. The biggest reason why they can't address them honestly is that they don't really understand the terminology and ideas at play. Many of them conflate omniscience with prescience. Prescience being the ability to know all possible future outcomes but not determinately, and omniscience being the ability to know the distinct and exact future with absolute determination.

From a biblical perspective, god is said to be omniscient and know the exact future with absolute certainty. We are told more than once that all things go according to god's will and that nothing can negate this. We're told that every plant and animal on earth bends to the will of god. This means that there are no accidents and there are no choices, but that everything is already predetermined and there can be no veering off the path.

If we look back at the original question and whether or not god can be truly benevolent and omnipotent and still tell a lie, we see once again two mutually exclusive ideas that negate one another. If you admit that god can lie, then you are saying he truly is omnipotent, but you negate any chance of god being strictly benevolent, because is god can lie, there is no guarantee that he hasn't lied before which would negate benevolence.

These sorts of paradoxes are some of the biggest contributors to people abandoning religion. When confronted with such ideas, many believers come to an understanding that we in this day and age understand these philosophical issues much better than those who wrote these doctrines. When we put that understanding to use, we see glaringly obvious flaws in the doctrine at a philosophical level. And if the doctrine is flawed at a philosophical level, we must question all the rest of it, and every philosophical idea within it.

7. Is observable physical evidence more important and valid than what the bible claims to be true?

Ken Ham and his Answers in Genesis foundation, have made the bold claim that the bible is the factual truth and that any scientific fact that disagrees with the bible is false no matter how much evidence there is to support science over biblical literalism. Their general stance is telling people to start by believing the bible and then to look at science and everything which seems to agree with the bible within a scientific framework is right, and that anything which disagrees with the bible is just wrong no matter what.

The reason this question is important is because it highlights the fact that these people can't be reasoned with or persuaded. It shows an innate bias with the believer that makes it impossible to have any meaningful dialogue with them. It also points out the fact, that while many believers, even literalists, will tell you they're open minded, the truth is that they aren't open at all to any idea which doesn't fit with their preconceived notions and personal bias. Ken Ham himself likes to chant the mantra of "were you there" in order to try and prop up his bias as a superior position. He claims that god was there and that god gave us the bible to tell us what happened.

The real problem with his fallacious argument is that even if we weren't there, we can still in fact know what happened. To illustrate how that can be, I'll point you to forensic science. You see, forensics itself is the act of taking what evidence that exists and rebuilding what happened based on that evidence. The most practical example of this is forensics within law enforcement. A criminal forensic team does not need to have been at the crime scene in order to know what happened at that crime scene. They can take evidence such as blood splatter patterns, DNA evidence, and use the laws of physics to determine things such as bullet trajectories or striking blow patterns, and they can piece together almost exactly what happened.

Within the scientific community, forensic anthropologists and geologists and biologists, do the exact same thing. They take all the evidence we have and they rebuild the crime scene, so to speak, to tell us to the closest degree possible what exactly happened. And like all scientific disciplines, forensic science advances every day.

The degree of accuracy with which we can make claims about past events grows each and every day along with our knowledge and understanding.

The real kicker here though, is the level of hypocrisy at play. You see, Ken would tell you that the bible is absolute truth and can provide all the answers you seek, and yet, if someone were to murder one of his family members he wouldn't just turn to the bible or to god, he would look to forensic science to give him an answer with real substance. If he were diagnosed with cancer, he mostly likely wouldn't just turn to the bible or to god in prayer. Instead, he would likely turn to medical science to help him survive. That same science he'd likely turn to, is greatly based on an evolutionary perspective of biology, which is something he claims is absolute nonsense. This level of unacknowledged hypocrisy is one of the greatest reasons that I and many others take these people like Ham and Comfort to task on their nonsense and try to expose the highly fallacious nature of their claims, and the hypocrisy of their actions versus what they claim to believe.

8. Is there any amount of evidence that would change your views?

Literalists love to pose the notion that atheists are closed minded and that they're actually very open-minded. Of course, like many of their other bizarre statements, the exact opposite is true. Many of them, Ken Ham and Ray Comfort included, have made it clear that there is no amount of evidence that could ever change their views. When asked what he'd do if it proven that god doesn't exist, Ray Comfort stated that he would pray to god for guidance. When asked what evidence would change his views on creationism, Ken Ham told Bill Bye that there wasn't any amount of evidence that would change his mind.

Of course, Nye didn't really have to ask this because it should be quite obvious. The reason I say this, is that there is so much physical evidence that a literal biblical perspective of human origins is false, that said evidence basically constitutes the whole of scientific knowledge. The fact is, that in order to hold to a biblical perspective on human origins, one has to either ignore or manipulate every bit of scientific evidence in order to hold to that perspective. The thing we all have to remember however, is that for fundamentalists like Ham and Comfort, this perspective towards science is necessary to validate their religious beliefs. For them, the Christian perspective only works in a literalist context.

This is why:

If the biblical creation myth isn't true, then there is no original sin. Without original sin, there is no need for Jesus. So each piece is dependent on the last for validity, and if you destroy the foundation the whole structure falls.

The reality is, that theologically speaking, they're absolutely correct. Any belief outside of the literalist perspective is tantamount to belief in elves or unicorns. It is belief without any valid foundation... otherwise known as faith.

It's odd how a real understanding of these ideas can clear up some misperceptions.

Do you remember how I said that biblical literalists actually worship the bible rather than god? Well, that idea is what is at play here also. You see, it seems that by following the literalist perspective they are more theologically sound, however the progressive Christian actually meets the requirement of god to believe by faith rather than proof. The same paradox that arises here, is the one which makes the no true Scotsman argument a fallacy. Theologically speaking, there's no true and valid way to say which position makes one a true Christian. So we must accept the notion that both are true Christians, and that the nature of Christian doctrine is such, that it allows for multiple interpretations and thus, for different schools of theological understanding. From that, we can gather that a claim of absolute truth by any Christian sect or denomination is fallacious and is based entirely on personal interpretation.

9. What physical proof is there that your particular god even exists?

With this one question I can destroy the notion of faith as it pertains to the biblical literalist.

You see, one cannot have both proof and faith. The two, as with many other ideas I've mentioned, are mutually exclusive. The reason for this is that faith is the belief in something which cannot be proven, so if you have proof you can't have faith because proof negates faith. No one needs faith to believe that which is proven to be true. The really tricky part about this however, is that the literalist tends to have a serious misunderstanding about what constitutes proof and what constitutes faith.

If you'll recall in question seven, I talk about how the literalist such as Ham makes the claim that the bible is absolute truth that trumps even scientific facts. That same claim is what is in play here, only in a slightly different way. You see, because of their claim that the bible is absolute truth, they in turn believe that the bible is absolute proof that their god exists. Because of this, the literalist has no faith in god, but rather believes he has proof that god exists. If they have proof of their god's existence, then there is no faith involved.

Now, one might argue that they have faith in the bible and that this allows them to still make a valid claim to faith. And that is when I will say that you're correct, but that this leads to a whole separate issue involving faith and idolatry.

Let me explain.

If a literalist wants to claim that they have faith, and that such faith is inherent in their stoic belief that the bible is the word of god, then I must point out that they are guilty of idolatry, for putting the bible before god. This takes a bit of explaining, but you'll see how it all works out. In order to get to that point, we have to understand a few theological ideas first though.

First, we must understand that god requires faith in him, not a book. When god supposedly tormented Job, there wasn't a book to confirm Job's faith. Job simply was expected to believe in god, and to simply accept that all things happen according to god's will. This is the faith that god supposedly expects of all mankind.

Secondly, we must understand that the bible makes it very clear that everything that mankind touches becomes corrupted and that all men are corruptible. Many supposedly righteous men have become corrupted and corrupted the things the touched, including ideas. This is all part of the concept of original sin.

Lastly, we must understand that the bible is a book written by men. And, that the men who actually wrote these books are not the men whose stories these books tell. At best, the accounts in the bible are second or third hand word of mouth stories put to writing. At worst, some of these stories span back generations as oral traditions until finally being written down.

Now, if we put all that together, we get the following theological idea:

The bible says that mankind is corrupt and corruptible. The bible was written by men, and so the bible cannot be fully trusted because men corrupt the things they touch, including ideas. So one must have faith in god over even the word of the bible and accept that the bible could be wrong about things even while still maintaining a belief in god. If a man puts his faith in the bible, then he's actually putting his faith in men rather than god, and he makes the bible itself an idol which they worship rather than god.

Now, if this sounds like circular logic to you, that's because it is. Outside of a biblical theological framework, this makes no sense whatsoever. Yet, within a biblical theological framework, the idea is completely theologically sound. The reason for this is that the bible's claim to authority is based on wholly circular logic. The bible is true because it is the word of god, and we know the bible is the word of god because the bible says it's the word of god. It's a snake eating itself.

This is why the bible is absolutely full of philosophical paradoxes, because each idea in it is only supported by itself. This is also why these philosophical paradoxes can be used to make the bible prove itself invalid. Any idea that can't be supported by outside evidence and facts, can ultimately be crushed under its own weight. This should make it obvious that the bible has no real philosophical merit. If we can use the bible to pose a philosophical argument that the bible isn't accurate, then what good is it?

10. Do you believe hell is a justifiable punishment for a simple lack of belief?

This one is also a bit of a trick question. The reason it's a trick question is because it asks them to address the question, not from a theological stance, but from one of personal ethical and moral understanding. In this question, I don't ask what the bible says about it, but rather how they themselves feel about it from a personal moral and ethical perspective. This question usually can't be answered honestly by the biblical literalist because they always want to refer back to what the bible says, rather than actually acknowledge their own personal feelings on the matter.

Many of the most hardcore literalists really do think this is a justified punishment, however many others still maintain a view of justice that tells them that this is morally wrong and unethical. And yet, even those literalists who know by their own conscience that this is wrong, still fight tooth and nail not to actually address that issue. They can't possibly address the notion that their god could act unjustly. But we're talking about an omnipotent being which means he should be able to lie and if he's able to lie then he's surely capable of injustice. Or maybe he is incapable of injustice and so he isn't omnipotent and not much of a god...

The reality is that almost all of us know through our own conscience that eternal damnation is not just. Even the Pope, leader of the largest denomination of Christianity on the planet, has said emphatically that this is not just. He's even offered theological discourse to try and justify the assertion that any good and decent person is deserving of heaven. Unfortunately for the literalist, this isn't a statement he can make.

I've begun to believe that heaven just wouldn't be as wonderful for the literalists if they can't also picture someone suffering that couldn't get in.

Part Two

Now, I want the reader to understand something here. These questions are not aimed at being a guidebook for attacking the Christian religion. In fact, these few questions fall short of accomplishing that goal by a good margin. If your aim is to shake a Christian's faith, then you'll need far more than this. The reason that these questions will not shake a Christian's faith is that, both literalists and progressive Christians can answer these questions. Many progressives can even answer them completely honestly, although you won't get any honest answers on much of anything from a biblical literalist.

The purpose of these questions is actually just to illustrate a point, which is that you can't actually reason with someone who has embraced insanity. The only way that you can ever hope to reach them is if you can first make them understand that they've embraced insanity and that these ideas are insane to begin with. The vast majority of progressive Christians have never even thought about just how insane these ideas are, and if they have addressed them at all it is usually by way of a minister or priest who has absolutely no interest in presenting them in an honest and unbiased way. I know people tend to think that their minister or priest is a trustworthy person, and in a general sense most of them truly are, but when it comes to theological issues they are completely biased on the matter and will almost surely never give any truly critical analysis of these ideas. Your pastor is not going to look at you and tell you that asking someone to murder their child is an absolutely insane and unethical thing for a supposedly benevolent being to do. For the most part they can't even see it from an objective standpoint at all.

Both the progressive and literalist start from the same flawed position, which is to first believe that god exists and then to go on to justify any supposed action or idea presented as being done or commanded by that god as being completely justified simply because it is claimed that this is what god wants. No matter how vile or wretched or insane the action or idea, if that's what god wants to do, or what god wants us to do, then somehow it becomes a totally moral and ethical thing in their minds. But when you bite the bullet and take the time to examine this from an objective standpoint, there simply is no way to say that a god who cannot even measure up to his own supposed standards can be called benevolent, nor is such a god worthy of any sort of reverence or worship if such a god were to exist at all.

You don't get to run around like a psychopath, asking others to join in with your madness, and then simply say, "Hey man… It's all good because I'm god." It is the acquiescence to such a fallacious notion that allows despots to commit horrible atrocities the world over since the dawn of civilization. We simply sit back and accept the absolutely false notion that the man who is *in charge* is allowed to do whatever he wants simply because he is *in charge*. But as we clearly see if we take a look at our history, at the great list of despotic rulers from our past, we are almost all sickened and repulsed by their actions, and nearly all of us make the judgment that those actions were entirely unethical. We must be willing to do the same with these ideas of god presented by these doctrines. We must come to an understanding that no one, not even a god if one should exist, is above or outside of the notion of ethics or morality. No one gets a *free pass*, and everyone must be judged equally on the merits of their actions.

Now, luckily for us this god of the bible is total fiction. Because were he not, our only options would be to worship madness or refuse and face eternal torture. As an atheist, I don't worry in the least about that imaginary punishment, however even if I knew for an absolute fact that it was true I still would not bow down and worship that tyrant. I would not make myself an accomplice to madness simply in the hopes that such madness would not fall upon my own head. Not only would such an exercise be totally futile because such madness always turns on everything around it as well as itself, but to become an accomplice to that madness would eventually drive you mad as well. *"If you dance with the devil, the devil don't change. The devil changes you."*

Of all the insanity in the bible, there is nothing and no one that even comes close to being as insane as this god itself. If you met this god on the street you'd turn and run the moment you saw the absolute madness in his eyes. This isn't madness like that of Hitler or Stalin, it's the sort of madness we see in the eyes of men like Charles Manson. It is a madness that lusts for blood and pain, and if no other idea within Christian dogma conveyed this, the concept of hell and eternal torture and torment most certainly does. Something that people simply don't want to look at is the fact that if we go back to those Old Testament books and remember all those babies murdered in the flood or during the many Jewish conquests ordered by god, that god damned them to hell by allowing their deaths under the assumption that they would be just as displeasing to god as their parents were. You can be sure that if hell were to really exist, it would be full of babies and children being tortured for all eternity. [3]

How can you possibly reason with someone who accepts the notion that god is allowed to do whatever he wants simply because he's god, which leads to all these other absolutely horrible and insane ideas like eternal torture for children based solely on their heredity? I don't honestly think you can reason with that at all, which is why this book is meant not for the fundamentalist and literalist who has descended so far down the rabbit hole of madness that they are simply lost, but for the progressive who may still possibly listen to a voice of reason. I'm asking you to turn away, not from the idea of god altogether, but from the madness which is religion and in this particular case Christianity. If you can just take an objective look at all this, I know that you can understand that you don't need that label if it means accepting all this insanity.

This is a call to those who can still be reached, and those who would listen. Just let go of this nonsense and all the trappings that come with it. You don't need it, and if you really think about it you probably don't want it either.

Chapter 6 :

A Final Plea on Behalf of Sanity

Now, undoubtedly there will be some who object to the use of certain terminology in this book. They will object to me using the term insane to describe these doctrinal ideas. Very likely, they'll object to my use of the term magic in reference to what they call miracles. I won't apologize for the use of those terms because to do so would be to apologize for simply being honest. Like it or not, belief in these things is in fact insane because to believe in them you must suspend rational thought. Whether you call it a miracle or magic, these supposed acts that are supernatural in nature are not rationally valid. The only difference between Merlin and Jesus is what they called themselves. One was said to be a great sorcerer and the other a miracle worker born of divinity, but in the end they both used supernatural abilities to manipulate the natural world which is by definition magic.

The greatest trick of religion is to make the unbelievable seem plausible by simple semantic arguments. They use words such as miracle to make magic seem plausible, when in reality these are just two peas in a pod. The names change, but the game remains the same. They ask you to deny the existence of Hercules as myth and accept that of Jesus as fact, all the while acting as though these two stories are not a mirror image of one another when in reality they are exactly the same. They argue for special pleading with no valid reason at all to do so, and all with nothing more than semantics and rhetoric that has no real meaning and that only seeks to obfuscate the issue. But when you invest the time to get to the heart of the matter and look at it objectively, religious belief is just as insane as belief in unicorns or leprechauns.

The only way to plead around all this insanity is to invoke the idea of faith. But the problem with this, as I've stated before, is that you aren't really invoking the notion of faith in god, but rather faith in men. Even when you say that these men were inspired by god, you are making that claim based solely on the claims made by other men. It is a circular fallacy which will get you nowhere. It leads from point A in saying that these men were inspired by god, to point B which says that this book tells us that these men were inspired by god, right back to point A which says that these men were inspired by god to make these claims that they were inspired by god. It's just a snake that is continually trying to eat itself. And we must all acknowledge that a snake eating itself is a most insane proposal indeed.

So here's the bad news for the moderate or progressive Christian; you're already failing at being a Christian. If you don't believe the bible from beginning to end, then you don't have the faith which the bible asks of you. If you try to cherry pick and use apologetics or shirk these ideas off as allegory, then you are attempting to change the supposed word of god. Did Jesus claim that the Genesis myth was allegory? Of course not, because to do so would totally undermine his claim to authority as king of the Jews. His very claim to kingship was through a lineage that supposedly stretched all the way back to Adam. Did he acknowledge that the supposed exodus of the Jewish people never really took place? Again, of course he didn't, because he needed all that to validate his supposed authority. If Jesus, who is said to be the son of god, believed these things as factual truths, and we must assume he did since he never once states otherwise and he also uses them to validate a claim to authority, then who are we to claim they are allegory?

There is this pervasive notion that the doctrine of the bible is open to interpretation, but that notion simply isn't theologically sound. The bible itself makes it very clear time and again that it says what it says and it means exactly that. It tells us time and again that god and god's will are unchanging and are not subject to the interpretation and whims of mankind. The will and desire of the god of the bible is the epitome of resoluteness, and because of this, belief in that god becomes an all or nothing proposition.

Now for the good news; even though you're failing as a Christian, you're winning as a human being. As a moderate or progressive Christian you've made a personal choice to accept a path led by the ethics of your own conscience. You've chosen to let go of those ideas present in the religion of Christianity which make it a divisive and hateful thing built on an irrational perspective of supposed superiority. You've chosen the philosophy of Jesus over strict adherence to arcane rituals and tradition. And I just have to say... I really love you for it, because the best kind of Christian is the one who wears the label more out of social convention than out of religious conviction.

But you're so very close to that moment of epiphany! You're just a few steps away, and I know you can see where this leads. That's the place you want to be, and that's the place people like myself need you to get to. You already don't believe the vast majority of these insane ideas and in all likelihood you're only holding on to these last few ideas in order to hold on to ideas which you find comforting. But all you're really doing is just lying to yourself, and you just don't need to do that.

I'm not asking you to take a leap of faith, but rather to leap out of faith. I'm not asking you to take my word for any of this, but rather for you to examine it for yourself. I'm not asking you to abandon the idea of god, but rather to abandon this religion because it is false. And honestly, so are all the other religions out there. There is nothing inherently wrong or evil about believing that a god exists, but when you choose to believe in a god offered by these doctrines you agree to all the insanity that comes along with it, and that most certainly is inherently wrong and evil, because it aids in vindicating all the insane people who actually do believe these insane ideas.

In an episode of The Daily Show with Jon Stewart, the religious scholar Reza Aslan made the claim that people wear the label of religion as an identifier of themselves. They hold to the notion that wearing that religious label is part of their self-identity, and honestly this is very true while at the same time being absolutely fallacious. You see, it is true because people do in fact believe it, but it is fallacious because when you get to the heart of the matter that label honestly tells me almost nothing about who you are as a person. You can tell me you're a Christian, but with over 30,000 different denominations of Christianity you may as well tell me that you like ice cream for all that says about you. At one point in history that label may have told me all I needed to know about you, but those days are long gone.

People in this day and age, whether they realize it or not, are defined by so much more than their religion or even their ethnicity and nationality. We exist outside of these rigid lines of ideology and are ever changing and ever growing, at least most of us are anyways. But we wear these labels because they're familiar and comfortable. We wear them because our parents wore them and dressed us in them as well. In the modern age the religious label is little more than costume jewelry that we wear out of sheer habit and social convention. But we don't have to and we need not lose any sense of identity by letting them go and shedding ourselves of what has become more of a burden than a comfort.

As a former Christian, these are ideas that I struggled through myself as I came to my current position as an atheist. The more time I invested in studying these things, the more I came to realize that I just don't believe in any of this nonsense. And as I came to understand my own doubts I realized that if I don't actually believe these things that there simply isn't any valid reason to wear the label. And when I shed that label it was like lifting a weight off my shoulders. I didn't have to lie to myself anymore and I didn't need to fake it to play a part that I wasn't truly committed to.

But you don't have to take it as far as I have. You don't need to become an atheist just because you don't believe all this religious insanity. If you truly feel that there is a god then hold on to that if it's what you truly feel and truly believe. But you already don't believe in the god of the bible, and there's no good reason to pretend that you do. You can believe in your very own idea of god. You can believe in a god who is not limited and defined by some insane doctrine. You can believe in a god who actually is benevolent and kind and loving, and one who doesn't supposedly torture people for eternity for not groveling correctly. You can believe in your god on your terms, and quite honestly most of you already do that without really realizing it.

If you ask ten Christians if they believe in god, they'll all tell you yes. But ask those same ten Christians to describe the god they believe in and you'll likely get ten totally different answers, because everyone's idea of god is rather unique to them regardless of what label they wear. So when you get right down to it, most moderate or progressive Christians are already well on their way to letting go of religion anyway. You just need a good reason to let go of those few threads holding you to it... and hopefully after reading this, you've got all the reason you need to simply let it go and walk away.

REFERENCES

[1]http://www.oxforddictionaries.com/us/definition/american_english/insane

[2] Deuteronomy 22:28-29

(All bible verses used in this work were gathered using the Bible Hub website.)

[3]http://www.atheistrepublic.com/blog/deandrasek/hell-children

AUTHOR BIO

Casper Rigsby is a 34 year old husband and father. He is the author of the bestselling title *The Bible in a Nutshell*, a prominent blogger at Atheist Republic, and a very vocal advocate for out of the closet atheism. His works seek to address fundamentalism at its roots through theological and philosophical discourse, which is also highly irreverent and often even blasphemous. His straight-forward and blunt approach can be abrasive to some and refreshing to others.

Other Books by Casper Rigsby

The Bible in a Nutshell

Atheisting 101

The Engineer's Argument

I'd like to say "thank you" for reading this book. If you enjoyed what you've read, then please take a moment to leave an honest review for my book. To show our appreciation for your support, when you leave a review for this book on Amazon or Goodreads, we'll send you a free copy of the book *Why There Is No God*, written by Atheist Republic founder, Armin Navabi, or any other book by author Casper Rigsby that is published through Atheist Republic. Simply send us a link to the review by visiting AtheistBookReview.com, and we'll send you a free copy of the book. Your reviews will help us reach out to more people who might benefit from this text and future material.

Made in the USA
San Bernardino, CA
25 October 2016